Joy Allan

Pastor Niyi Adebayo
Jesus House Aberdeen

THE MIRACLE

OF THE CITY OF GOD

The Miracle of City of God - Secrets of God Construction Site

© 2011 School of Wisdom Publishing House

ISBN 978-1-908327-01-7

Printed in the EU

JESUS HOUSE @ CITY OF GOD
THANKSGIVING

To the Lord Most High.
Our Gratitude, Praise and Worship is in the words of David.
Like David we are the recipients of God's great goodness:

I will extol the LORD at all times; his praise will always be on my lips. I will glory in the LORD; let the afflicted hear and rejoice. Glorify the LORD with me; let us exalt his name together.

I sought the LORD, and he answered me; he delivered me from all my fears. Those who look to him are radiant; their faces are never covered with shame.

This poor man called, and the LORD heard him; he saved him out of all his troubles.

The angel of the LORD encamps around those who fear him, and he delivers them.

Taste and see that the LORD is good; blessed is the one who takes refuge in him.

Fear the LORD, you his holy people, for those who fear him lack nothing.

The lions may grow weak and hungry, but those who seek the LORD lack no good thing.

Come, my children, listen to me; I will teach you the fear of the LORD.

Whoever of you loves life and desires to see many good days, keep your tongue from evil and your lips from telling lies.

Turn from evil and do good; seek peace and pursue it.

The eyes of the LORD are on the righteous, and his ears are attentive to their cry; but the face of the LORD is against those who do evil, to blot out their name from the earth.

The righteous cry out, and the LORD hears them; he delivers them from all their troubles. The LORD is close to the brokenhearted and saves those who are crushed in spirit. The righteous person may have many troubles, but the LORD delivers him from them all; he protects all his bones, not one of them will be broken.

Evil will slay the wicked; the foes of the righteous will be condemned.

The LORD will rescue his servants; no one who takes refuge in him will be condemned.

– Psalm 34 (NIV)

From the Pastor, Ministers, Men, Women and Children of God in the Jesus House City of God family 2004 to 2011

Prayer

PRAYER BY PASTOR ENOCH ADEBOYE

(GENERAL OVERSEER OF THE REDEEMED CHRISTIAN CHURCH OF GOD) DURING THE DEDICATION OF JESUS HOUSE'S CITY OF GOD COMPLEX

"We pray that beginning from now, this place shall become a miracle centre. We pray that every sinner who would step into this place will be saved. Every sick person who will enter this place from now will be healed. We pray that every captive who will ever set his or her foot into this place, Lord will be set free. Father we pray that if they bring the dead here, the dead will rise in Jesus name. We pray Lord Almighty that every prayer said here will get instant answers. My Lord and Saviour, we pray that the lost glory of this particular building will be restored. From here my Lord and God, the fire of revival that will sweep throughout Scotland will start afresh in Jesus name. Lord I pray that all your children who are here now will carry additional blessings from you in the name of Jesus. Everything they touch from now onwards will prosper in Jesus mighty name. All the people Lord that you have used for the purchase of this building and all that you will yet use for the renovation, my Father and my God bless them Lord, meet all their needs, let it be well with them. I pray that every one of us will be there with you to reign on the last day. Thank you my Father, glory be to your holy name even as we dedicate this place to you in the name of the father, in the name of the Son and of the Holy Spirit. AMEN"

Table of Contents

Credits

PUBLISHER
School of Wisdom

CHIEF EDITOR
Pastor (Dr) Mark Osayomwanbo Igiehon

EDITOR
Uche Okorji

CONTRIBUTORS
Alero Igiehon, Ame Utiome, Jide Odunlami (Nigeria), Tobi Adegoke (Nigeria), Femi Labeo-dun, Idongesit Umoh, Sola Okunuga, John Abolarin, Pearl Digwo, Iyalla Ibiyekariwaribiribo, Iyiola Ogedengbe, Obinna Njoku, Niyi Adebayo, Kunle Akinlalu, Segun Akinkugbe, Eniola Onafowokan, Uzezi Obaro-Okpopkor, Friday Aniefiok, Alaba Edebiri, Kingsley Anao, Sope Scott, Onyedikachi Zubi-Emele, Janett Obot, Ivana Akaraiwe, Chidinma Oriunuebho, Tolani Akinlalu, Jide Olatinsu, Joe Ochie, Wale Oni, Demola Agunbiade, Daniel Arojojoye, Efe Obaro, Emilia Nnoji, Dolapo Faturoti (nee Tade), Jimi Akande, Femi Akarakiri, Uchechi Uche Dibiaezue, Sandra Stewart, Marvis Amadi, Michael Dada, Tosin Emilorolun, Solomon Akare, Kenechukwu Njoku, Raymond Eli, Ayo Akintomide, Dapo Olarenwaju, Richard Amadi, Kemi Arojojoye, Damilola Soyingbe, Bukola Faturoti, Jennifer Abayowa, Roland Okocha, Funmi Adetunji, Morenikeji Oni, Wahabi Giwa- Osagie, Modupe Ologunieko, Azu Osuagwu, Roland Okocha, Funmi Adetunji, Idara Akpan, Lucky Anuopogena, Dapo Olowodaran, Chuma Okoronkwo, Hyacinth Meze, Christy Surtees, Ngozi Vincent-Eloagu

MATERIAL COLLATION
Uche Okorji

ART DIRECTION/ DESIGN/PRINT
Sayitbetter Media - The Branding Guys
[admin@thebrandingguys.com]

Dedication

To the Lord Most High and
Every Soldier of the Cross

As the end approaches, the dealings of God with His body "The Church" becomes apparent and the need to spread the news to all living things becomes even obvious. This documentation of God's dealing with Jesus House Aberdeen in the last seven years is dedicated to every soldier of the cross (every Christian) around the globe.

Following the Acts of Apostles in the Bible, we have tried in this book to carefully compile with accuracy a faithful record and testimony of God's goodness in Jesus House Aberdeen; to serve as an encouragement to the Church of what God can do and the blessings that come with serving him faithfully.

We at Jesus House Aberdeen are honoured to be part of God's move in this end time and we encourage everyone as you read our testimony to put your hands on the plough and work more with God the Master of the Universe.

We wait to hear and rejoice in your testimony. Great is the Lord and greatly to be praised!

Foreword

Praise to the Most High God

Now to Him who has done and continues to do exceedingly abundantly above all that we could ever (even in our highest prayers, desires, thoughts, hopes or dreams) have asked or thought, according to the His glorious power that works in us, to The Lord Most Eternal be glory in the Church by Christ Jesus to all generations, forever and ever. Amen. (our rendering of Eph 3.20-21)

WHY THIS ACCOUNT?

Luke 1. Forasmuch as many have taken in hand to set forth in order a declaration of those things which are most surely believed among us, [2] even as they were delivered unto us by those who from the beginning were eyewitnesses and ministers of the Word, [3] it seemed good to me also, having had perfect understanding of things from the very first, to write unto thee in order, most excellent Theophilus, [4] that thou mightest know the certainty of those things wherein thou hast been instructed.

Firstly, because it is fitting and proper to diligently record the great deeds of our great God that more glory and honour may be given to Him.

Secondly, it is necessary that a good account be rendered of the acts of God through this His Church. Posterity needs to know what great things the Lord did in and through His people in this generation.

Thirdly, because, the kings, the high and mighty in society have heard of some of the great things that the Lord has been doing through this part of His Church and are eager to learn of the details of the testimonies and good reports.

And the king talked with Gehazi the servant of the man of God, saying, "Tell me, I pray thee, all the great things that [God] hath done." 2 King 8.4

Fourthly, as testimonies are infectious, we know that this Book of Testimony shall be God's instrument to push great many lives and churches and cities forward mightily.

Fifthly, we want to document the little that we have come to know about God's ways. We are God's projects; we are in His construction site and are recording some of what we are learning as workmen in the Lord's vineyard.

Sixthly, , this account is because we appreciate that our present is nothing compared to where God is taking us (Eph 3.20). Like Paul, we thank God for how far He has brought us; yet we know that we have only just begun. There is the whole race of life which we must keep running and complete successfully at the feet of the Most High. We press forward, therefore, to enter into the welcome of His warm embrace in Heaven. We press forward into His higher calling for our lives and His church and put old things, even these testimonies - behind us, renew our faith and press forward anew.

Finally, our testimonies ensure that we may commit ourselves again to the Lord, and put heaven in remembrance concerning God's people who have been instruments for His works these past seven years. This book will be the book of permanent remembrance for every good that they have done towards God, His Church, His people and the land. The Lord will remember and bless everyone He has used and continues to use as His army for this end time work.

INCREDIBLE GOD

The records of the Lord's deeds always make for a fascinating read. For us at Jesus House and the City of God, it has been and continues to be incredible living in God's great goodness, and in the era of His mighty moves and tremendous blessings. The Lord has wrought great things since the Church commenced in 2004 as a parish of the Redeemed Christian Church of God.

As we move into the Seventh Year, the Sabbath Year (Lev 25.1-5), we want to declare to the highest heavens how good, how faithful, glorious our God is. We want to boast the loudest to our generation that our Lord is the best! Since our inception, we have seen lives transforme for the Lord; souls changed and changing from hopelessness to hopeful; we have seen great healings – cancers, HIVs, barrenness and all of manners of sicknesses; we have witnessed the births of numerous babies in a land where the birth rate is declining; we are witnesses of how the lowly and rejected have been divinely promoted to high places; we have seen the poor ushered into places of wealth; we have seen the unmarried ushered into divine matrimony and we have seen the confused receive divine direction. It has and continues to be awesome what the Lord is doing in Jesus House and at the City of God.

What shall we say about the forceful advance of the Kingdom of God – the kingdom is advancing forcefully across Aberdeen, Scotland, United Kingdom and Europe – incredible. We have seen those who thought "God was dead" humbled by expansion and His great doings through His Church. To Him be glory!

MOMENT OF INTERCESSION

What shall we say of God's people? I bless You dear Lord and Father, for your people, incredible people, precious people, people that you loved so much that Christ died for at the cross of Calvary. Your people in Jesus House at the City of God are wonderful and caring. They care about you Lord. They are striving to get closer to you. They care about your kingdom; they make sacrifices for the kingdom. They travel far and wide to see your kingdom established in places – far and near; that is not common.

They are striving to pray more, study more, and teach more. I love your people. They make mistakes, we make mistakes but you always help us to find our way back on track.

I thank you Lord that your people are givers - your church is a giving church. I love your people. Please, Lord bless your people again for the good they continue to do to your Church. Your people are wonderful: they do church, they attend church, and for their sake You are in church every time we come together – what a wonderful story. Hebews 10.25

God's people make Him look good (2 Chronicles 24.16, Luke 10.21)

- The Word is working in their lives. Hard cases become glorious testimonies.

- They are the church: Matt 18.20

- Anyone who comes here will become a compulsory believer in miracles.

- The Word says prosper and they prosper.

- The Word says be fruitful and they are incredibly fruitful. Anyone anywhere desiring to be fruitful – get close to God's people in the Jesus House family and you will become mightily fruitful

- The Word says give and your people are incredible givers. 1 Chronicles 29.8-end

- The Word says bring all the tithe into your store house and your people are incredible tithers. Anyone who believes in tithing will become a believer in Jesus House.

- The Word says marry and marriages are plenty among your people O Lord! Your people marry well and enjoy their spouses and families. Genesis 26.8, Proverbs 5.19

- God's people in Jesus House at The City of God Family, dress well, honouring the Lord with their bodies. Others see them looking good for God and the Lord is glorified. Ecclesiastes 9.8

- God's people in the house are incredibly hospitable; they can entertain angels and the Lord. Lots of celebrations and parties – always celebrating the Lord's goodness

- God's people are reaching out to the wider society through welfare outreaches; encouragement ministries, joyful ministries. Lord bless your people again and again and again!

- God's people really do enjoy themselves – football games, picnics, hill-climbing, children's activities, Thank God It's Friday (TGIF) outreaches, music concerts, Gospel Battle of the Bands: they are showing the world how great fun-filled and joyous, it is to walk with the Lord. Those who say the Lord is hard and terrible become converted when they see how much fun happens in Jesus House at the City of God. It is good to serve the Lord

CITY OF GOOD REPORTS

We see transformations under God daily. In this place, in this Church, we the people here see lives that were hopeless turned to the Lord and completely turned around; terrible diseases including terminal cancers healed; turnarounds for marriages and relationships previously headed for the cliff; lives without purpose turned to purposeful and impactful ones; our music teams bringing hope and joy and renewal to many in free outdoor and indoor concerts across Aberdeen and the cities of Scotland; we see hearts and right values being restored in lives and so many other great reports. Great things are happening in God's churches and the land through the Church!

KINGDOM OF RECORDS

God's kingdom is a kingdom of records. The Bible is the greatest record-book spanning accounts for over 6000 years and counting and covering the beginning (Genesis) to the end of time and creation (Revelation). Heaven's records are complete and exhaustive. In the Bible and in Heaven there are records of those who present themselves before the Lord (Job 1.6, Hebrews 10.25); records of alms, gifts and charity to the poor and needy (Acts 10); records of prayers as incense and of those who pray (Acts 4.23-31); records of those who responded to the call for repentance and revival (Mal 3.16-18); records of those who did exploits for God and His Kingdom (1Chronicles 11; the Acts of Apostles); and detailed records of those who built God's dwellings (Nehemiah 3). Hence, the essence of our records.

OUR RECORD, OUR STORY

In this book, we have sought as much as possible to present a record and account of some of the great and faithful deeds of God and His people through one part of the Redeemed Christian Church of God, the Jesus House Port Harcourt and her missionary parishes in Europe. Our record cannot in any way be as comprehensive and complete as Heaven's records. If we have missed any record, we know that Heaven has the perfect record. This is the record of the missions established in Europe by RCCG Jesus House Port Harcourt firstly Paris' La Maison de Jesu (Jesus House Paris) and Jesus House Aberdeen (The City of God) and the off springs from them as at June 2011.

INTO ABUNDANT AND EVER INCREASING GRACE

Have we started yet? Of course not! We know God has only just begun with us. This is just the beginning. Our goal for each one of us is Heaven. We will pursue holiness and righteous-living until we get home. We will walk with Him until we are translated home to the Heavenly City. We will under Him do great kingdom exploits until the Kingdom of God rules in our generation (1Chronicles 11).

This is a compendium of the testimonies of:

RCCG Aberdeen: City of the Great King, Smithfield

RCCG Aberdeen: Jesus House Dyce

RCCG Aberdeen: Jesus House @ The City of God

RCCG Aberdeen: Jesus House Torry

RCCG Budapest, Hungary: Jesus House Budapest

RCCG Edinburgh: Edinburgh Tabernacle

RCCG Elgin: Elgin City Tabernacle

RCCG France: Peace House, Fountainblue

RCCG France: Cite de Dieu, Marseilles

RCCG France: La Maison de Jesu, Paris

RCCG France: La Maison de Jesu, Rouen

RCCG France: Le Havre Cite de Joyeux

RCCG Glasgow: City of God

RCCG Inverness: Jesus House

RCCG Montrose: Montrose Tabernacle for All Nations

RCCG Perth: Perth City Tabernacle

RCCG Sterling: City of God

RCCG Watford: City of God

RCCG Wick: City of the King

With God in us, we will - more than Solomon ever did - display the Excellency of our God to our generation. We pray and desire to become a veritable end time army for God, greater than David's army and do more exploit than did Paul and the people of old.

We are the sheep of His pasture. To Him Alone be all the glory, honour, majesty and thanksgiving. We appreciate You Lord for the opportunity to live and walk with you and work for you.

Mark O. Igiehon

Mark Osayomwanbo Igiehon

Introduction

As I write this section of this book I count myself privileged to be part of the testimony of Jesus house. I am also humbled that God has chosen me to spear head, write and put together the history of His church, Jesus House. I count it as a big privilege and I believe the Lord has been preparing me silently over the years for this task as I joined the church a year after its commencement and have been a part of the great testimonies. I equally witnessed and was a part of most of the phases the church has been through, starting with the days of few numbers in Torry to what the church has become today.

At the start of this project, one of the scriptures that Pastor Mark discussed with me was Luke 1. With emphasis on how Luke carefully examined and searched out the truth of the gospel and how he reported his findings to most excellent Theophilus of his time. In the same vein, the information on the history of Jesus House as well as the dealings of God with the church have been carefully gathered and put together. This book has been written in the place of careful gathering of detailed information, much time with Pastor Mark Igiehon and other leaders and pioneers, with so much study of the word and prayers.

This book has been designed and written as a historical report but one with a twist. It incorporates traditional history told with a unique style in presentation, Bible exposition and a style of writing that will come across as captivating,

> 'This book has been designed and written as historical report but one with a twist.'

intriguing and fun. Each chapter tackles a part of Jesus House family history, testimonies of God's great wonders in the church and in the life of members.

Another main component in each chapter is the testimonies of members which have been written to edify and encourage everyone that would read this book. It is then wrapped up with the lessons we have learnt from the dealings of God based on the topic of that chapter; hence the book's sub title: "Secrets from God's Construction Site".

The secrets which we have learnt from our dealings with God do not apply only to the church. They are written so that we can incorporate the secrets (lessons) in our lives, careers, church and all other spheres of life. The secrets from God's Construction site at the end of each chapter are also very much applicable in our lives as individuals. They are truths that would put you above your peers. I encourage you to prayerfully read them and ask God to reveal to you the facts that you need for your life to be made perfect.

We are also mindful that this book would go beyond the four corners of our church into the hands of those who are involved in other ministries and churches that would like to pick up some principles that Jesus House has learned and is using. Hence, we have put down the writings of this work in such a way that it would benefit those in that category as well. It is my prayer that the Lord will reveal to you from our experience as a church the tools you will require for this end time move of God.

I count this history work as a fun book to read and I promise you that there will not be a dull moment as you go through the pages of this book. Finally, I also pray that the good Lord will bless everyone that goes through this book and reveal to them the things they would need in their sojourn on earth. I equally pray that the Lord will keep you to the end and for a festive welcome in heaven.

Uche Okorji

Chapter 1

IN THE
BEGINNING...

"When we look back; these last 7 years, we can clearly see that God has favoured us (Jesus House), we see His goodness, provision and mighty hand. To Him alone be all the glory."

Aberdeen is a city that historically typifies the long-standing relationship between God and man, known for her exploits in kingdom business, and witness to the thriving ministries of such kingdom generals as John Knox, Mary Slessor, and James Kidd. You can scarcely work down the streets of the Granite City without seeing a church or the remains of architectural icons that once stood-out as church building. History has it that the Gordon Highlanders - who marched in defence of the king, used to march down Aberdeen's Union Street, in their full regalia Sunday mornings to church.

Furthermore, Sunday evenings, saw Aberdonians in great throngs to witness great debates between a profound Bible scholars of their time, Rev. Dr. James Kidd and other ministers in the city, within the Union Street area. So great was the relevance of the gospel that families in Aberdeen made it a point of duty to pay for pews in the church which would be reserved for members of their family to seat whenever they attended service.

Aberdeen used to be a commercial nerve centre; generating a large chunk of its income from fishing and the University of Aberdeen which dates back to the 16th Century. However, it was the discovery of crude oil in the North Sea during the early 70's crude that brought the city to the limelight as the oil capital of Europe. Sadly, as the society became more industrialised, Aberdonians lost sight of the need for God in their lives, turning rather to human government for sustenance and support. They thereby, exchange the love of the Most High God for human illusions such as lusts, pandering of all sorts, drinking, drug abuse and inevitably domestic abuse and violence.

It is from these ashes of despondence and despair that we fashion our tale, history, challenges and testimony of how God has started and sustained his work in Aberdeen making it a source of light to reach out to the other cities in Scotland and Europe as a whole.

THIS IS OUR STORY

"Visiting the Calabar Museum, Nigeria in December 2003, was both a sobering and an awe- inspiring experience. For it is impossible to miss a large section of the museum dedicated to the life and ministry of Mary Slessor in large parts of South Eastern Nigeria. Mary Slessor was born in Aberdeen and in her early years relocated together with her family to Dundee, from where she was sent by the Church of Scotland to South- Eastern Nigeria as a missionary. So mighty was her impact in the land that the fruits of her ministry still endure today. It is a unique opportunity and privilege to join in the work of propagating the Kingdom of our Lord in Mary Slessor's home town and country."

– Pastor Mark Osayomwanbo Igiehon

In 2003, according to God's divine plan and purpose, Pastor Mark Osayomwanbo Igiehon was sent from Port Harcourt, Nigeria with his family to Aberdeen. Prior to leaving Jesus House Port Harcourt (Nigeria), his home church, he was commissioned to set up a Jesus House parish in Aberdeen by Pastor Charles Adegoke -the Provincial Pastor of Rivers Province (Nigeria) at that time and the then Zonal Pastor, Pastor Songo Barango.

On arriving Scotland in June 2003, Pastor Mark worshipped with the Redeemed Christian Church of God, Fountain of Love serving under the leadership of Pastor Chris Gbenle. During this period, he was focused and believed God to start up an arm of the Redeemed Christian Church of God church according to the mandate given back in Nigeria.

Eventually, Pastor Mark met with some brethren interceding for the land of Aberdeen and praying for revival to break forth in the city of Aberdeen where godlessness seemed to be the order of the day. They not only prayed, but also evangelised, preparing the land for what God was set to do. These brethren of like passion included Gbite and Nike Falade, Chris and Joy Iheobi, John Alamu, Echefu Ezenwa, and Udo Udo. Irrespective of commitments in their various local assemblies, they met on a weekly basis in line with God's admonition in Genesis 11.6 that if brethren gather and be of one mind that there was nothing that they imagined to do that could be restrained from them.

Pastor Mark Igiehon continued to seek God's face on where and how to go about the planting of God's church. It was in the place of prayers that the Lord laid it upon his heart that he should go to a part of the city of Aberdeen known as Torry: a community famous for its fishing prowess in the past that lies on the south bank of the River Dee and in the words of an Aberdeen-based pastor, "a very challenging place".

These circumstances notwithstanding, the servant of God, Pastor Mark Igiehon

forged ahead with the leading of the Holy Spirit.

To the Glory of God, Jesus house Aberdeen had her first service at Torry on the 6th of June, 2004 with 6 people in attendance, three adults and three children: one of whom was Caleb Ogbouche, from Jesus House Port Harcourt, who had determined that he would be at the first service whenever the church starts. He also sowed into the new mission work and returned to Port Harcourt after the first service which was a prayer and praise service in a basketball court at the Torry Community Sports centre, Oscar Road, Torry.

The number of original attendees was increased at the second service again with the coming of Jimi Akande; a worker in Jesus House Port Harcourt, who was miraculously transferred to Aberdeen from his place of work. Similarly, on the third Sunday, the Lord added the Akimoladun family to His church.

The church was inaugurated on Sunday the 4th July, 2004 by Pastor Raymond Eli and the church service held at the Sports centre until the Lord led Pastor Mark Igiehon to

EXTRACT OF AN ARTICLE FROM 'THE CITY OF GOD' MAGAZINE, SUMMER 2008

PICTURES OF THE FIRST SERVICE AND THE OTHER EARLY DAY'S

Pastor Chris Gbenle ministering in Torry

change the location of the church in Torry in September 2004. The location was changed to the Balnagask Community Centre, Torry. This proved to be a timely decision as this would have been a great challenge for church services to continue to hold there with the setting in of the winter months. Interestingly, after the church moved, the sports centre was closed temporarily for major renovation. Presently, the Community Center houses a branch of the Jesus House Parish. The church of God grew, went forward, waxed strong and became greater to the Glory of God, confirming God's word in Matthew 16.18 that He will build his church and the gates of hell will not prevail against it.

Pastor Mark Igiehon ministering

Some members fellowshiping

To the Glory of God, the Lord used the different challenges the church encountered as an avenue to reach out to people. In the early days, a challenge the church was faced with was the lack of venue for services during the Christmas period, as the Community Centre was closed during these periods. As a result, the church used the St Fitticks Church in Torry during these periods. This provided the opportunity for the church to establish a good relationship with the St Fitticks church. We were then able to the use of their facilities for Christmas services, communion services and choir rehearsals. This also provided opportunities to worship with them and the Salvation Army at other times.

JH Choir at Salvation Army Christmas Concert December 2006

Choir Performance at St Fitticks Church of Scotland 2006

The question was asked, why Pastor Mark Igiehon would go ahead irrespective of the existence of a Redeemed Christian Church of God (RCCG) parish at the time of his arrival in the city. Thankfully, the answer is not farfetched; according to the RCCG mandate under the leadership of Pastor Enoch Adeboye, a key goal is to plant churches within five minutes driving distance in every city and town of the developed countries. This paved way for the vigorous church-planting activities and mission works launched out by the church. Noteworthy is the immense support the young church received from Jesus House Port Harcourt as well as the Fountain of Love Church, Aberdeen.

HE HAS DONE GREAT THINGS

The Lord blessed His church tremendously in various ways. For example, He added unto His church the first baby, Tony, born to the family of Brother Azu Usuagwu.

PASTOR MEZE

Still in those days, the Lord blessed His church with a wonderful woman in the person of Ms Hazel McAllan. She is the administrator of the Balnagask Community Centre used by the church in Torry. Being a local, she introduced the church to several new ways to reach out to the local community. She invited the children's church to perform a dance at the annual Torry Gala. That way, the name of the Lord was made known to the people of Torry in their local setting. Our God, in His Wisdom, spread His fame abroad through the children's performance which led to the invitation of the children dance crew to open the Live8 Conference at the Aberdeen Exhibition Centre on the 6th of July, 2005. To the glory of God, it was a huge success as the name of the Lord was exalted and His church was advertised in the local newspaper and in the city.

In the early days, the Lord used a lot of lives to bless His church. The children church was started by Sister Uzezi Obaro-Okpokpor. She became the first Children Church pastor and remained so until her relocation to Port Harcourt, Nigeria. Shortly before the move, however, she handed over the children church to the Sis Ngozi Vincent-Eloagwu who still pastors the children church today. As part of reaching out to the children in the community, the church was also involved in an outreach to the Torry Academy.

The outreach was targeted at giving the children in the academy good role models to look up to rather than look out in the secular world. In order to achieve this, members of the church shared their experiences in life, what their careers entailed and how they had progressed over the years. Furthermore, the children were taught gospel songs and the word of God through quizzes, this way the church gave back to the community.

Church members manning the stand with Pastor Meze at the Gala

The children performing at the Torry Gala 2005

Jesus House Stand at the Gala with Pastor Meze 2005

Torry Gala participants helping themselves with refreshments

Mummy Folu Akimoladun was another woman of virtue the Lord used to bless His church. She was a mother to everyone. She always had students come over to her house for lunch on Sundays. She equally gave out food packs to the young students in the church at the time.

Apart from that, she was heavily involved in the follow-up of members; a pressing need of the church at that time. She did this diligently and voluntarily, seeking no reward until she relocated to Nigeria due to the promotion of the Lord. She also hosted the church's prayer group in her home at that time every Monday in the evenings. Because the prayer team at that time consisted almost entirely of students, she picked and dropped off brethren before and after the prayers up till the time of her relocation.

Upon her relocation, the fellowship that held at her house was moved to the home of Jimi Akande whose wife Toun Akande served as the host.

The prayer house grew and a time came when it was hosted by different homes including those of Obaro and Uzezi Obaro-Okpokpor, Jolomi Adams as well as Solomon Akere. After Mummy Akimoladun, the Lord raised Himself Dapo Olanrewaju (formerly Dapo Nurudeen), a man committed to prayers, to take charge of this unit and is still the pastor in charge of prayer.

Uzezi, Obaro with the church

Newsletter LIVE8

Jesus House Children opening the LIVE8 concert in Aberdeen, July 2005

Monday, June 19, 2006   FUN IN FOCUS TORRY GALA AND MEDIEVAL FAIR SPECIAL   29

REVVED UP: Ethan Niven tries out a motor bike.

BIG SMILES: Kai and Kelsea Warzala.

SCARY: Charlie Johnstone.

ENTERTAINING: Members of the Redeemed Christian Church.

HAVING FUN: Fron left, Owen Simpson, Anne-Marie Baillie, Kim Boyne and Andrea Elliott.

Gala day was great success

TORRY GALA

TORRY people arrived in their droves to the enjoy the annual community gala on Saturday.

And despite the wet weather, there were smiling faces all round as music and dance groups entertained the visitors who came in their hundreds.

And River City actress Joyce Falconer, who officially opened the event, impressed onlookers with her hand-written poems about Torry.

One of the organisers Sheila Thomson said: "I am always amazed by Torry people. I thought the day was going to be a disaster because of the weather but there were about 600 people altogether. There was a great mix of entertainers and together they made the day a great success."

RING THE BELL: Max and Rachel Milne try their luck at one of the stalls.

VROOM: Shantelle Birdi with grandad Michael Forbes.

REGAL: Rachel Duncan and friend Emma Holmes, both 5.

HEAD-DRESS: Eva Milne with Michael Beckett.

JESTERS: Banchory VC haveing fun.

Crowds flock to mediaeval fair

ST TERNAN'S MEDIEVAL FAIR

FROM ferret racing to fighting displays and banqueting – Banchory enjoyed all the fun of the mediaeval fair at the weekend.

Locals and visitors were lured to the St Ternan's Fair by the saint himself, ringing his bell around the streets.

And despite the dull weather a steady stream of revellers turned for the event held to celebrate the founding of the town by St Ternan, a fifth century abbot.

Banchory and District Initiative development officer Evelyn Crossan said they included a wide range of attractions including the Mediaeval Realm re-enactment group's tented village, a sit down banquet, fighting displays and ferret racing championship. More up-to-date offerings included a van powered by bio-diesel.

WAR-LIKE: Matthew Burnie with 'David De Brownhill', left, and 'Sir Tristan Moore'.

ON THE BALL: Banchory VC's captain Lorne Taylor controls the ball.

CAMPER: Milly Judt from Bavaria.

ON THE BALL: Dominic O'Donnell gets hockey tips from Hazel Cowan.

Or view and order pictures online at www.thisisaberdeen.co.uk

The Evening Express report on the Torry Gala

DEDICATION OF JESUS HOUSE
ABERDEEN 4TH JULY, 2004

A Message from Pastor Ray Eli

Text: Acts 8.1-8

And Saul was consenting unto his death. And at that time there was a great persecution against the church which was at Jerusalem; and they were all scattered abroad throughout the regions of Judaea and Samaria, except the apostles. And devout men carried Stephen to his burial, and made great lamentation over him. As for Saul, he made havock of the church, entering into every house, and haling men and women committed them to prison. Therefore they that were scattered abroad went everywhere preaching the word. 5Then Philip went down to the city of Samaria, and preached Christ unto them. And the people with one accord gave heed unto those things which Philip spake, hearing and seeing the miracles which he did. 7For unclean spirits, crying with loud voice, came out of many that were possessed with them: and many taken with palsies, and that were lame, were healed. 8And there was great joy in that city.

Persecution of the early church resulted in the spread of the gospel of our Lord Jesus Christ. From the book of Acts 8.1-8, we learn about the man Philip, one of the 12 disciples of Jesus.

He went about carrying out the great commission given by Jesus Christ before his departure from earth according to Mark 16.15-18.

All Philip did was to go into the city and preach the gospel. Because of his obedience, God backed his actions with results and there was great joy in the city. For us today, as the church and body of Christ, we have to carry on with the great commission and mandate reaching out to all nations, cultures and languages. This is the reason why this church has been planted, so that we can reach out to our neighbourhood.

The only qualification we need for preaching the gospel is to have a relationship with the Lord. Only then can we reach out to the people by sharing our testimonies with them. Our testimonies will speak for us as they will show forth the goodness of the Lord, magnify his awesomeness and draw men to Him for they will want to partake of the goodness of God. Finally in his closing remark, Pastor Ray Eli admonished the church to reproduce a church of all nations, languages and cultures. This has been the aim and testimony of the church.

TESTIMONY REPORTS

JESUS HOUSE ABERDEEN: THE EARLY JOURNEY

- Jimi Akande

At the end of Oscar road in Torry, Aberdeen is the Torry Community Sports Centre. Its basketball court sits 200 comfortably, but on June 7th, 2004, six people gathered to hold the very first service of Jesus House Aberdeen, a parish of the Redeemed Christian Church of God.

The church's mission statement was clear. We were in Torry to preach and teach about the one true God, win souls for Christ and touch the lives of the people in Aberdeen. Saturday evangelism took us to every pub, betting house; every nook and cranny in Torry. Every house or flat in Torry received at least a copy of the Jesus House tracts.

We met both born-again Christians and those requiring help: backsliders, drunks, clairvoyants, atheists, the afflicted, jobless and the divorced. Prayers were made to redeem the lost as that's what it was all about- Souls!

By September 2004, we moved over to the Balnagask Community Centre, also in Torry, as the sport centre was to undergo some renovation. We faced some initial challenges. The church banner erected every Saturday evening was constantly brought down. Initially it was taken away but later, the culprits would walk to the church and return the banner. Definitely, God was touching those lives.

One of the initial prayer points for the church was for God to bring in the labourers, as the harvest is plenty. Since then, we have witnessed the hand of the one true God (Is 43:10), the God of "suddenly", the God of "open doors", the God of resurrection, the Mighty Warrior, the God of the impossible, the incomparable God, the Lord Almighty is His name. God has gradually moved the church from good and towards great as God's blessings have been evident.

JIMI AKANDE

Below are some of my learnt lessons from the journey thus far:

Go with what you have and God will definitely bless you with more: We kicked off all necessary church programmes despite our size: Sunday school classes, Children's class, Bible study. As the labourers trooped in, so did the harvest. Holy Communion service held on the first Tuesday of each month and a 'Good Life fellowship' was held every Thursday in a pub or restaurant.

Missions and church planting is a must. Through our limited finances, the parish birthed Jesus House Inverness and Jesus House Budapest and is supporting them fully.

Make it a goal to let the larger community know there is a church in the neighbourhood: The church's presence began to spread to the greater Torry community. The church was invited to the Torry Gala (2005 and 2006) where the children's choir gave a remarkable performance. The children's choir also performed at the LIVE 8 concert in 2005. We have had outreaches in Torry (schools), Banchory and Dundee. There is now a dedicated evangelism team.

Cultivating an attitude of expectancy: Though the church may have started small on the outside, in the inside it was growing and we had a vision.

The journey this far has been the journey of faith. Glory to God!

GOD IS FAITHFUL AND TRUST WORTHY

- Alero Igiehon

Great is God's faithfulness to us and I say this with all my heart. No one else but God Almighty could have organized our entry as a family into Aberdeen in the United Kingdom. In His humorous way, God decided to give us a preview of Aberdeen in March, 2002; a year before we knew we would be coming over to Aberdeen. Therefore, when I arrived with the family, I knew this was a place of destiny and that great testimonies will abound. Suffice to say that my testimony and that of my family is that God is so trustworthy. He continues to keep us in perfect peace andprospering His work and us too beyond our imaginations.

I must not fail to testify of the abundant grace of God that has humbled me, prepared and empowered me to carry out the many assignments that I have had to do (sometimes in the face of adversity) towards the expansion of God's Kingdom in Aberdeen. By His Grace, I pioneered the choir until it was handed over to Obinna Njoku. There were the days of participating in evangelism with one desiring to win souls for Christ. What joy it was to be a part of this great work then and now!

It has been a wonder to see how our Lord has transformed lives for the better in Jesus House; with the unsaved becoming saved and so passionate for God, and with the hopeless becoming not

ALERO IGIEHON

only hopeful but victorious. Indeed there has been great advancement of the people of God and His church and this is set to continue until the Day of the Lord.

The conclusion is that God Almighty who is Yahweh is so faithful and requires that we serve Him with all our hearts, souls, minds and strength and great shall be our prosperity.

GOD'S GREATNESS, POWER AND MAJESTY

– Obinna Njoku

I clearly remember arriving Aberdeen on a cold September morning in 2004 for my MSc. Studies. The windy chill was not welcoming as I made my way through the cabin of the plane down the stairs onto the tarmac. Single and with an exuberant heart, I knew my coming to Aberdeen was God's plan, though I knew no specifics.

This story is not about me but God; His Power, greatness, Majesty, Mercies and Love. It's just over six years from the first day I arrived Aberdeen and I want to share some great testimonies of God.

When I arrived in Aberdeen, God quickly made me understand that my aim of coming was to support the Kingdom's work. I had been involved with the choir back home (Nigeria) and had a little knowledge of playing the keyboard and so I started working in Jesus House Aberdeen, which

was then about 3months old with about 12 adults and 6 children. I also became the church treasurer and had other ministerial and administrative roles.

At that time, God started opening doors for the church to minister in schools, fairs etc. On one occasion we went over to Torry Academy and taught the kids gospel songs and played quizzes, a seed was sown! We started working with the local community and became a regular feature at the yearly Torry gala.

OBINNA NJOKU

Peniel, our annual conference, kicked off in 2006 and has continued to grow from strength to strength. The choir then made the local press and Journal news paper for the music concert held at the beach ball room as part of Peniel 2006. Again God started to move us beyond the borders of Aberdeen to Inverness and Budapest which were the first mission parishes we opened and which - by God's Grace - are doing great today.

From a congregation of 20, God moved us to close to 150 in 2008. One thing was evident in the focus and passion of the workers; God brought faithful labourers knowing the harvest was plenty. We have continued to grow spiritually, numerically, financially and improved the quality of service to God and his people. We have since acquired two separate worship complexes in Aberdeen worth a total of £1.6m. The work is far from over as we reach the people of the land through the strength of the Lord...*For by strength shall no man prevail.*

The bible says God rewards our labour of love. There were and still are abundance of testimonies; Students getting blessed with good jobs, singles finding life partners, babies coming in their numbers. God is Faithful!

As for me the once single man – God has blessed me with a wonderful, virtuous and beautiful wife Kenechi and two great daughters Michelle and Joanne... Yes I am out-numbered. God has also blessed me with a very good job, health, worthy friends, joy, peace and more than I asked for.

If I was asked 'if I would do it again i.e. give my time and energy as before' my answer would be yes, a 110%.

I encourage you to serve the Lord with your heart and strength, living an obedient and holy life and the benefits of son-ship will be yours on earth and in heaven.

Jesus House Aberdeen Torry Days

JESUS HOUSE JANUARY 2005

CHURCH DECEMBER 2005

Children's Day 2007

New Year Celebration Service - January 2007

Church Service 2008

SECRETS FROM GOD'S CONSTRUCTION SITE

From the inception of Jesus House Aberdeen, a great deal of lessons has been taken on by the body of Christ. These lessons (secrets) have taught us and still reveal to us more about God, His power at work in our lives, as well as His sufficiency and tremendous miracles. Some major lessons are highlighted as follows

● Despise not the days of little beginnings

The church started that with three adults and three children has steadily grown over the years, under God's watch and tender care. In the seven years that have gone by, God's house has witnessed tremendous breakthroughs to the glory of the Father.

"And though your beginning was small, yet your latter end would greatly increase." Job 8.7 (The Amplified)

From the passage above we see that God is committed to making our future prosperous no matter how little our beginning may have been. The Message translation puts that verse of scripture as: "Even though you're not much right now, you'll end up better than ever". So no matter how you feel about where you are right now, always know that God has a better tomorrow for you. He says in His word:

I know the thoughts I have for you, thoughts of good and not of evil, to give you a hope and an expected end. - Jeremiah 29:11)

For my thoughts are not your thoughts, neither are your ways my ways, saith the Lord. Isaiah 55.8 (KJV)

The Lord has good thoughts concerning us. He is a good God and has the best in mind for us. In everything we do, let us always remember that the future is brighter than the past. When God wants to do great things, he looks for humble people that he can work with.

● We are destined for Greatness

'And we know that all things work together for good to them that love God, to them who are the called according to his purpose.

For whom he did foreknow, he also did predestinate to be conformed to the image of his Son, that he might be the firstborn among many brethren.

Moreover whom he did predestinate, them he also called: and whom he called, them he also justified: and whom he justified, them he also glorified.' Romans 8.28-30 (KJV)

From the scripture, we see that all things work together for the good of those who are called according to his purpose. Hence as his children, all things will work together for our good because we love God. He already has destined us for great things as long as we love Him and remain in His purpose and will.

The verse that follows shortly after says: *'What shall we then say to these things? If God be for us, who can be against us?' Romans 8.31 (KJV)*

This scripture assures u that because God is on our side, no one can be against us. Therefore we should not entertain any fear. He has destined us for great things. The book of Isaiah 8 vs 18 confirms that we are created for signs and wonders to our generation. Can you beat that?

● God can confound the wise through the little and seemingly foolish

From just three adults and three children, God has brought glory to Himself by expanding the work in multiple folds, and yielding fruits of increase in the hundreds.

'... and upon this rock I will build my church; and the gates of hell shall not prevail against it.' Matthew 16.18b (KJV)

God can use little things to do great things. No matter how little we might think of ourselves and our resources, God can magnify it. He can expand our little efforts and make them very great. All He requires of us is our willing hearts. He searches the deep things of our hearts to judge our faithfulness. He definitely rewards good and faithful people no matter how lightly we seem to esteem ourselves as it is written, *"He uses the little things of this world to confound the wise"*.

■ CHILDREN CHURCH JAN 2008

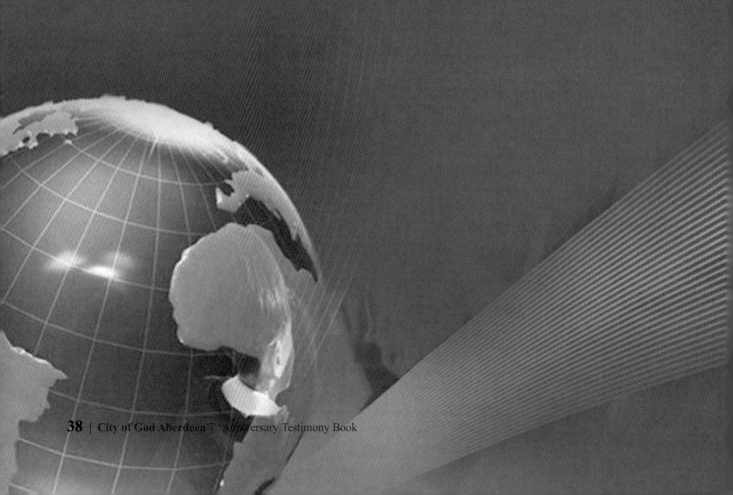

Chapter 2

THE
ANTIOCH CHURCH

"Now they which were scattered abroad upon the persecution that arose about Stephen travelled as far as Phenice, and Cyprus, and Antioch, preaching the word to none but unto the Jews only. And some of them were men of Cyprus and Cyrene, which, when they were come to Antioch, spake unto the Grecians, preaching the LORD Jesus. And the hand of the Lord was with them: and a great number believed, and turned unto the Lord." Acts 11.19-21 (KJV)

"Now there were in the church that was at Antioch certain prophets and teachers; as Barnabas, and Simeon that was called Niger, and Lucius of Cyrene, and Manaen, which had been brought up with Herod the tetrarch, and Saul. As they ministered to the Lord, and fasted, the Holy Ghost said,

Separate me Barnabas and Saul for the work whereunto I have called them. And when they had fasted and prayed, and laid their hands on them, they sent them away." Acts 13.1-3 (KJV)

Jesus House Aberdeen grew in the hundreds and waxes stronger today. Once internal consolidation had been attained by the church, the need to enlarge the place of her tent became paramount. Therefore, as was the case with the church in Antioch, the leadership began to wait on the Lord; seeking His will on where to go and establish the next arm of God's Kingdom. It was during this period of waiting that the Lord directed His church to Inverness that effectively became a type of our first fruit.

THE FIRST FRUIT OF INCREASE: JESUS HOUSE INVERNESS

Inverness is the major city in the Scottish highlands and a tourist hotspot. During a prayer visit to Inverness on the 8th of April, 2006; Pastor Mark recalls what may be aptly described as a miraculous encounter with an Invernessian gentleman which confirmed the leading of the Lord to start a mission in Inverness. The vision for taking on Inverness for the Lord, thus, was actualised after a weekend outreach: evangelism and dinner. This work commenced immediately under the supervision of the pioneer parish pastor, Hyacinth Meze, who was posted from the Aberdeen church.

Jesus House Inverness opened its doors for worship on Sunday, the 16th of April 2006. Since its inauguration, the Lord has

Church Service at Inverness church

Group photo of the Inverness church
during the first anniversary

Pastor Mark conducting
water baptism in Inverness

Inverness Church music outreach
in the streets 2007

Christy Surtee enjoying Sola Okunuga medley

been faithful and the Church has grown steadily. The Lord went ahead of His Church and has blessed her with dedicated members who have been vessels in the Lord's Hands and committed to His work. The Lord has sustained the work and performed great miracles in the midst of His Church at Inverness.

After its first year of inception, the church was blessed under the leadership of different ministers including Idongesit Umoh, Niyi Adebayo, Peju Deekae and now Wahabi Giwa-Osagie.

The work at the church was boosted by the efforts of church workers who travelled from Aberdeen on Friday nights or Saturday mornings for evangelism, follow-up and visitation. These workers included students who were willing to sacrifice their weekends and resources for the work. In return, God prospered their lives with amazing testimonies as they faithfully worked for Him.

THE MACEDONIAN CALL: JESUS HOUSE BUDAPEST

Indeed history repeats itself in various ways. To a large extent, the story of Jesus House Budapest bears some semblance to Paul's work at Macedonia as recorded in Acts 16.6-9.

Now when they had gone throughout Phrygia and the region of Galatia, and were forbidden of the Holy Ghost to preach the word in Asia, After they were come to Mysia, they assayed to go into Bithynia: but the Spirit suffered them not. And they passing by Mysia came down to Troas. And a vision appeared to Paul in the night; There stood a man of Macedonia, and prayed him, saying, Come over into Macedonia, and help us. Acts 16.6-9 (KJV)

Original found in COG magazine attached pg 13, 2008

Some Inverness Foundational Mission Crew:
Inewari, Deola, Kingsley and Onyedikachi.

Historical records indicate that most Hungarians became Christians as far back as the 10th century when Hungary's first king, Saint Stephen, was converted to the Christian faith. The communist era (1945-1986), however, was a major setback to the Christian faith in Hungary. Nevertheless, through our budding ministry, a lot of Hungarians today have rededicated their lives to God and accepted Jesus as Lord and Saviour.

Our story of Jesus House Budapest is thus:

A student, Emilia Nonji, from Budapest, Hungary came to Aberdeen in December 2005 on Christmas vacation during her which she visited Jesus House in Torry. As a result of her encounter with the Lord at Jesus House Aberdeen, she requested that the church comes to plant a branch in Budapest, Hungary and thus began the journey.

The mission work started as a fellowship at a member's home and was inaugurated on the 6th of May 2006 by Mark Igiehon. The work so prospered and grew that a need arose to move to a bigger venue. To the glory of God, on the 30th of September 2006, the church moved to a hall. The mission, currently, is supported by Sam and Janet Dennis.

Hungary Church started
as a House fellowship

Anniversary Service at
Jesus House Budapest

THE HUNGARIAN CHURCH OUTREACH

SECRETS FROM GOD'S CONSTRUCTION SITE

The speed at which God has moved His church – building a mighty army for His end time move – is simply amazing. Many lessons we are learning and secrets that have unravelled regarding what God can do with and through missions are as follows:

• God delights in First Fruits

A vital lesson we have learnt as a church is that the first fruits of all our increase belong to God. This spiritual principle is typified by God's willingness to sacrifice His only begotten son in order that we might live. God is interested in our first fruits and when we give it to God he blesses us more mightily.

• God is able

One of the things we have learnt as a church is that our God is able. All He requires from us is to step out in faith and He will carry us through. As a church, we stepped out in faith into the unknown (Inverness) and God carried us through and today, the Church of God is standing to the Glory of God.

• God's hand is a safe haven

Another secret we have learnt from God is that whatever we entrust into His hands, He is faithful and just to keep. All the churches, we have planted have been committed into God's hands and we have come to understand and see that, He has always kept all that we have committed into His hands. Indeed He has kept His churches.

From this, we have learnt as a church to hand over all we have into God's care. This way, we are rest assured that He will preserve all that concerns us unto the perfect day. It also means that we do not need to worry about what would happen to our possession. He is the only guarantee of safety we have and need. We should also entrust our lives into His hands because in His hands we are secure and safe.

Chapter 3

TIMELESS RHYTHM!!!

Art, a product or process of deliberately arranging elements in a way that influences the senses or emotion has been a vital tool God has used through the church in reaching out to the community. Being a language that everyone understands and easily associates with, the forms of art: music, dance and drama have been employed by the church as a tool for evangelism to reach out to lost souls as well as minister to the brethren in the fold.

SPEAKING A UNIVERSAL LANGUAGE

Music which is an art universally accepted by all cultures has been a major instrument which the church uses to reach out to the people.

From the beginning of our missions work this has been a tool that the Lord has used to reach out to people of different backgrounds and personalities. Starting from Torry, the church became actively involved in the activities of the local community. It all started with the annual Torry Gala of which the children church were always in attendance to sing and dance. To the glory of God, this outing led to the church gracing the pages of the North East Scotland's Evening Express (June18, 2006; page 29) and an invitation to the children's group to the LIVE8 concert.

THANK GOD IT'S FRIDAY (TGIF)

The music outreach went on to a new level when the Lord laid it in the heart of a church worker, Sister Vivian to start up an outreach aimed at reaching out to the community especially the youth community through music. So, Thank God It's Friday (TGIF) was started with the sole purpose of lifting the Lord in the city centre through music, singing and dancing on Friday evenings. This created a fun atmosphere to worship the Lord and engage the folks positively, drawing them to the light. A lot of lives have been reached and ministered to through this outreach. It has been a medium to take the gospel close to the youths who would on a normal day not go to church. Through this outreach as well, the Lord has made His work known in the city.

Still on music, the Lord has used the church music team to bless the church and community. The choir has grown so much and different music groups have evolved out of it including the City of God Choir, Aberdeen Gospel Mass choir, Jazz Ensemble, Jah Gos'pel. These music teams have ministered in different ways to different groups of people. The choir has had collaborative ministration and events with the Salvation Army and has been invited to minister at different events such as weddings, senior citizens homes and company end of year events.

JH choir ministering during the inaugral service of City of God

Book and Resource stand at TGIF
outreach Easter 2007

TGIF Outreach: Demola, Tobi and Iyalla dancing
to the music during the outreach

JH praise team ministering on
the 1st sunday in year 2009

JH choir minstering during the annual conference Peniel 2009

Group picture of JH choir after the inaugural service of City of God in 2007

Panel of Judges at Battle of the Bands

Music group ENGRAVED Winner of Battle of the bands 2009

THE BATTLE OF THE BANDS

The church has long strove to get the youth involved in gospel activities and the things which pertain to God. This was achieved in some respect when the Battle of the Bands was born in 2009. This outreach encourages the youths and bands in Scotland to get to know God and search the scriptures. The outreach required local youth bands that enrolled for the competition to search the scriptures and compose original lyrics for their songs from the Bible. This encouraged the youths to get to read the Bible and bring out lyrics that would glorify God. Prior to the performance, the different bands had to submit the lyrics to the team in charge for ap-

Shola performing during an interlude at the Battle of the Bands

Pastor Mark and Councillor Alan Donnelly
at the Battle of the Bands

proval after which they performed and competed amongst themselves. Partnering with the church as a co-sponsor was Bruce Millers; the winning band took away a cheque of one thousand pounds (£1000) from the church while the first runner up went home with musical equipment from Bruce Millers.

Based on all these music outreaches, the Lord has made His praise known in the city and different news media carried these good news including the press and journal.

MINISTERING THROUGH DANCE AND DRAMA – THE KINGDOM THEATRE

Another tool that the Lord has used to reach out to the community through His church is the kingdom Theatre. This is a group that ministers through dance and dra-

Kingdom Theatre ministering during a church service

ma at numerous open air crusades and outdoors events. They have been an active group that work with the TGIF, ministering in dance and drama. The kingdom theatre also has an annual programme called EXCEL; ministering the word through dance and drama. The EXCEL program has been a success and many lives have been blessed through it.

At the start of the Kingdom Theatre, Pastor Mark commissioned Helen Omole (nee Igene) to start the group. Later she handed over to Halima Akinkugbe now wife of Glasgow's City of God pastor. On Halima's relocation to Glasgow to join her husband, the leadership was succeeded by Ikenna Monyei who has moved the ministration of the Kingdom Theatre to a new level. Today, the Kingdom Theatre works creatively in presenting the gospel of our Lord Jesus Christ in an inviting, appealing and appreciative manner.

SECRETS FROM GOD'S CONSTRUCTION SITE

It really is amazing to know that God uses everything to glorify Himself. The works of art understood and appreciated by many have been used by God to open our eyes as a church to so many things about His nature and personality which we often ignore. Our God is all knowing and indeed worthy to be reckoned with. By the use of the works of art by the almighty, the church has learnt some secrets from God.

● God has the key to every man's heart

This is a vital lesson we learnt: that God has a key to every man's heart. He said in His word in Psalms 24 that all that is in the earth belongs to him.

> *"The earth is the Lord's, and the fullness thereof; the world, and they that dwell therein." Psalm 24.1(KJV)*

Hence, every human being on the face of the earth belongs to Him. If we all belong to him then, he knows each and every one of us and the way to reach out to us. He said in the book of Proverb 21. 1:

> *"The king's heart is in the hand of the LORD, as a the rivers of water; he tur-*

neth it whithersoever he will." Proverbs 21.1 (KJV)

Who can know the heart of a man?

If the heart of a king is in His hands, then that means that He actually knows about every one of us and hence, understands how to reach out and minister to us. We also understand that the Lord searches the deep things of the heart and knows the mind of men.

We see that God can minister to some through music, some through dance, some through drama, and some through the word; the list is endless. He has a way to reach each and every one of us. One thing we take from this is that we should be sensitive as missionaries, ministers or workers to understand the mind of God so as to understand the way God wants us to minister to our community.

As a church we have learnt to explore all the opportunities and ideas God has given us so as to win many for Christ. Apostle Paul speaking said:

> *"For though I be free from all men, yet have I made myself servant unto all, that I might gain the more. And unto the Jews I became as a Jew, that I might*

gain the Jews; to them that are under the law, as under the law, that I might gain them that are under the law; To them that are without law, as without law, (being not without law to God, but under the law to Christ,) that I might gain them that are without law. To the weak became I as weak, that I might gain the weak: I am made all things to all men that I might by all means save some." 1 Corinthians 9.19-22 (KJV)

As a church, we, like Apostle Paul explore varieties of ideas and opportunities to become so many things to different people so as to win souls to Christ.

• Music can glorify God

Sing joyfully to the LORD, you righteous; it is fitting for the upright to praise him. Praise the LORD with the harp; make music to him on the ten-stringed lyre. Sing to him a new song; play skillfully, and shout for joy. - Psalm 33.1-3

O clap your hands, all ye people; shout unto God with the voice of triumph.

Sing praises to God, sing praises: sing praises unto our King, sing praises.For God is the King of all the earth: sing ye praises with under-

standing. - Psalm 47. 1, 6-7

Oh that men would praise the LORD for his goodness, and for his wonderful works to the children of men! - Psalm 107:8

Another lesson we have learnt is that music is heavenly and glorifies God. From the passages above, we see that we should praise God through music and singing. The bible makes us understand that the Lord inhabits the praises of His people. Music is heavenly; the angels in heaven constantly glorify God.

• Evangelism requires Creativity

As a church we have also learnt that our God expects us to be creative in broadcasting and marketing His gospel. We have to be creative in packaging what we offer to people. One important thing we have noted is that people take interest in things that are well packaged and presented. Since we have the precious gospel we ought to deliver it to our community in a refined way that would cause them to be interested in serving God. If we show is presented in an exciting and attractive form, people would want to be a part of it. But if presented in a boring, unattractive form, they would not want to be a part of it. Hence, in our generation and time, the Kingdom Theatre and the various music groups aim to present the gospel to the people in an attractive form.

● Praise and worship will open shut doors

Yet another lesson we have learnt is that God can use praise and worship to open doors. When we praise and worship God the Lord opens the heart of the people. One profound thing we have seen through the ministry of the TGIF and the different music groups is that when we worship God in spirit and in truth, God opens the doors to the hearts of the people. At this point they want to be part of that genuine experience, thus creating an atmosphere to minister to them the gospel.

● Yokes will be broken through godly *music*

Another thing we have learnt in the cause of our work with God is that when we lift his name on high, yokes are destroyed because evil forces cannot stand the presence of God. The Bible makes us understand that the evil one flees at the mention of the name of Jesus. There is absolute surrender to the power of the Holy Spirit when God is lifted up. We use music, praise and worship to lift up our God in the city so that God can have his way and do as He pleases in the lives of His people.

EXCEL NITE AT COG CAMPUS, SMITHFIELD

ABERDEEN MASS CHOIR INAUGURATION CONCERT

Chapter 4

WILLING AND AVAILABLE VESSELS

Our God - the Lord of the harvest - always prepares for Himself vessels unto honour to do His work; a major testimony the Jesus House group of parishes is very thankful for and an indication of God's manifold wisdom. This has over the years ensured that God's work is constantly progressing and that the gates of hell cannot prevail against it. A typical example of God's provision of willing and available vessels is the church administration which was solely administered by volunteers at the onset until the church grew so much that there was need for workers attending to the business of the church on a full time basis.

Apart from the administration, most of the missions were started by people who volunteered to go to the mission fields every weekend to do the business of the kingdom. Most of the missions and parishes established by the church had the underground work carried out by willing vessels; selfless in their service to God.

THE BIRTH OF A MIRACLE: CITY OF GOD, GLASGOW CHURCH

In 2007, the Lord laid it in the heart of his servant, Pastor Mark Igiehon, to start a mission in Glasgow. In other to achieve this goal, he sent a two-man missions team to start the "City of God" parish, Glasgow. Thus began an incredible adventure that has shown God's faithfulness and favour. The two-man team consisting of Taiwo Ogunsanni and Segun Akinkugbe was later increased by one with the inclusion of Bro Emmanuel Omuederiaye.

of worship. After a night of prayers, God led us to the Junction Bar in the heart of the city centre where we were granted a lease of the first floor hall. We held a prayer vigil ahead of our first service, asking God to prosper the work, and since then the pace at which the work has progressed has been outstanding." – Pastor Segun Akinkugbe (Parish Pastor)

City of God Glasgow outreach team after outreach 2007

City of God Glasgow having service at Junction Bar

The first service had 6 people in attendance and today the church has grown in numerical strength and influence in the city of Glasgow.

THE TIMOTHY GENERATION (TIMGEN)... REACHING OUT TO THE STUDENT COMMUNITY

The campus community is yet another arm of the church that has benefited from the selfless administration of God's children who have – like Peter – let go of their resources and said to the Lord: 'You can use my boat'.

The work was started by Uche Okorji and a lot of students have been used by the Lord to support the work and advance the work as leaders. These include: Damilola Soyingbe, Angelo Nwigwe, Lolade Balogun, Oberhiri Solomon Otakore and Offiong Orok. The fellowship has the vision of building students to be like Timothy: the biblical character that was commended by Apostle Paul for his faith and encouraged to continue in holy living and service to God; preaching the word and leading by example. TimGen reaches out to the students' community in various ways, sharing the good news to the student community.

Seeing that students are the potential leaders of tomorrow, the fellowship continues to look for varieties of media to reach out to these young ones to ensure they are fed and inculcated with the knowledge they need for the future.

Group picture after TimGen's End of
Session Get-together 2010

TimGen lunch 2009

Despite the challenges, the Lord remained faithful and has sustained His work in the fellowship. Today, the fellowship runs in University of Aberdeen and the Robert Gorden University.The work has been supported by a lot of ministers including Tosin Emilolorun, Mark Igiehon, Dapo Olanrewaju, Mark Stone (of Elim Church) and Joe Ibojie (of Father's House Aberdeen). The fellowship also had her members from the churches in Aberdeen not just Jesus House.

BIBLE STUDY WITH KOLA BOLANTA AT GLASGOW CHURCH

SECRETS FROM GOD'S CONSTRUCTION SITE

These are some of the lessons we are learning as a church on the availability of workers.

God will use willing and available vessels

God is always looking to use available, obedient, honourable and willing vessels. We see from 2 Timothy 2.19-21, that in God's house there are different kinds of individuals considered as vessels. We can either be vessels unto honour or unto dishonour. The criteria for being a vessel unto honour is that one purges himself or herself and is sanctified for the master's use.

It is clear also to learn that for God to use us as vessels unto honour, we would have to be prepared. A vessel that will be used is one who is willing and submitted to the authority of Christ. Therefore, God expects us to be ready and prepared for His use; only then can he consider us vessels unto honour.

Besides, in my devotion to the temple of my God I now give my personal treasures of gold and silver for the tem-ple of my God, over and above every-thing I have provided for this holy temple: three thousand talents of gold (gold of Ophir) and seven thousand talents of refined silver, for the over-laying of the walls of the buildings, for the gold work and the silver work, and for all the work to be done by the craftsmen. Now, who is willing to con-secrate themselves to the LORD today?" – 1 Chronicles 29.3-5 (NIV)

From the scripture above, we see that David offered his best for the building of the Lord's temple and gave his personal treasures. We need to give our all and our very best to the Lord. This act of giving makes vessels unto honour to our God.

God rewards diligence

Now he that planteth and he that wa-tereth are one: and every man shall re-ceive his own reward according to his own labour. – 1 Corinthians 3.18 (KJV)

But without faith it is impossible to please him: for he that cometh to God must believe that he is, and that he is a rewarder of them that diligently seek him. – Hebrews 11.6 (KJV)

In as much as God is willing to use faithful men that are willing and available, He is also committed to rewarding them. As we invest into His work, He invests into our lives to carry out good works and to be filled with all His goodness. He is very careful to bless those who allow Him to use them in His work to His Glory.

From the text, Hebrew 11.6, we see that God is a rewarder of the diligent. He requires us to believe in Him for the things that he wants to do through us and for us. God does not want us to feel cheated after we have invested our time, resources and intellect in His work. Therefore, He promises reward for the faithful and diligent.

TIM GEN

Chapter 5

THE BARE NECESSITY OF JESUS HOUSE

"Every true prayer is a prayer of the church; by means of that prayer the church prays, since it is the Holy Spirit living in the church, who in every single soul prays in us with unspeakable groaning." – Unknown

Over the years Jesus House has grown through the power of prayer. In the days of the apostles, the prayer house was a top priority for the church. Prayer is a very important part of the christiandom as Jesus counsels us saying: "...men ought always to pray and not lose heart." Luke 18.1 (KJV)

Understanding this reality and principle, Pastor Mark Igiehon made it a priority. As earlier mentioned in chapter 1, the birth of Jesus House Aberdeen came as a result of much prayers. This led to the formation of the prayer team that was first led by Mummy Akinmoladun in the early days. On her departure the mantle was handed over to Dapo Olanrewaju. At the inception, the team met once a week to lift the church before the throne room, offer prayers and praise and also intercede for the land of Aberdeen.

The Bible says that: *"The effectual fervent prayer of a righteous man availeth much."*- James 5.16 (KJV).

The prayer team grew and raised mighty men that stood in the gap on behalf of the land of Aberdeen and the church. Soon the team extended her influence to the whole of Scotland. This led to the birth of the Flying Squad. The Flying Squad includes men with one purpose and that is to go from city to city every month to pray and evangelise sowing spiritual seeds to be reaped by the body of Christ in that city. Through the leading of the Holy Spirit, they are led to different towns and cities in Scotland. This team was started and led by Ayo Akintomide.

Through the Flying Squad, the work of the Lord has increased in Scotland as it has led to the birth of different missions (churches) including Elgin, Montrose, and now Perth. To the Glory of God these parishes are standing strong. Apart from the flying squad, the Lord brought great miracles in the church through the prayer team.

EFFECTIVE FERVENT PRAYERS - THE BIRTH OF ELGIN

As the prayer squad went from city to city under the leadership of Ayo Akintomide, the Lord did great and mighty things through them and a lot of testimonies were birthed through this outreach, chief among which is the birth of Elgin City Tabernacle. This is what Ayo Akintomide has to say:

"We thank God for the vision of the Jesus House Prayer Flying Squad which led to the establishment of the parish in Elgin. The Squad was commissioned to go from city to city in Scotland to pray and evangelize, thereby preparing the grounds for the fulfillment of God's plan for these cities in terms of salvation of souls and establishment of new parishes.

The first visit of the Prayer Squad to Elgin was in October, 2008 where we found a good spot at the city centre to pray, worshiping God in praise, dance, and evangelism. A man approached us after we had finished praising and dancing and expressed his admiration, seeing people worshipping God the way we did. He said he would have to travel about 15 miles for an opportunity to have that kind of encounter. We considered his enthusiasm as a confirmation from

the Holy Spirit that we should quickly raise an altar where God's name shall be glorified in the city.

At the first ministers' meeting in 2009, Pastor Mark indicated that the parish in Elgin must start in the first quarter of the year. We visited the city a couple of times to continue our prayers and to get a convenient location for the parish and God helped us, as we were able to secure the community centre and held our first crusade on Saturday March 28, 2009. The crusade was a huge success despite a heavy downpour; we had the full support of the Production Team and the workers-in-training as well as Pastor Mark Igiehon and Pastor Biyi Adeniran from RCCG Kings' Court, Airdrie in Canada.

The first service in the city was held on Sunday March 29, 2009 with eleven people in attendance including one visitor who God has now fully established in the parish. The visitor, on the second Sunday, said he was at the crusade and was amazed at seeing people defy the rain to praise God in the open. One other person said he has been to a lot of churches, but he felt more at home when he worshipped with us. God has continued to draw people to himself every Sunday and we pray He will establish them fully. We truly appreciate our God for these testimonies and we know He will do much more than we can ever imagine as we continue to lift His name high. Praise the LORD."

The church has continued to grow and to the Glory of God more than 50% of the members are Scottish. A lot of testimonies have come forth out of this seed. Today the church is under the leadership of Daniel Arojojoye.

Choir singing and dancing during
the Elgin Anniversary lunch

Elgin church group picture 2010

TESTIMONY REPORT

RESCUED BY GOD

– Sandra Stewart

When Jesus rescued me many years ago, it began with the knowledge that God loved me so much that He sent His only Son to die that I might live. Although I'd been taught this as a child and had felt a stirring in my heart, it was when I finally surrendered after many years of resisting that I found the peace and joy I'd long for; which the world could not give me. Thus began my Christian journey, as time and again God proved His faithfulness and goodness in so many ways. Now as I look back on my life so far, it is clear that every of my step has been ordered, and that every experience with God prepares me for the next step along the road He planned. With that assurance I could I never doubt that His way is best.

God's love is unconditional- even with all our faults and failings His love for us never changes. Receiving and experiencing this love is liberating and we are set free from guilt through the sacrifice of His precious Son on the cross. Forgiveness is granted because of His grace and mercy which is abundant and freely available.

All of this is ours to have; because we receive freely, we should freely give as well. Joy fills our hearts as we discover how bountiful God's love is, and our response should be to gladly share this joy with others in any way possible.

Christianity is not about rules which bind and hinder, but about discovering and knowing the Person who is the source of all joy.

The world looks on and so often fails to see the exuberance in Christians, and so make up their minds that these holier-than-thou people are hypocrites, and that the Church is a place you go to after you've cleaned up your life. This hurting world needs to hear the message of hope as people struggle with problems daily, and we should be living out the answer found only in Jesus.

Sometimes this way is difficult, but Jesus identifies with our struggles, and tells us to cast all our cares on Him for He cares for us. He endured the pain of the cross for the joy that was set before Him. He encourages us to look at the bigger picture.

Someone once said that when a fly lands on a famous picture all it can see is the tiny fly view of where it's landed. But in order for us to appreciate the painting in all its beauty we have to stand back and appreciate the work of the Master. We can be so utterly consumed by our circumstances that we cannot see, or even dare to believe that the Master has already applied the finishing touches to the masterpiece of our lives. He alone knows the end from the beginning.

I was that fly on the painting, allowing hurt and disappointment to overwhelm me, and seeing only the problem with very limited vision. I could not see the bigger picture from

where I was. In my heart I knew God wanted me to talk to Him. I also knew from experience that there is power in praise, and that battles have been won simply by praising His name.

Where was my Joy? The joy that had sustained me in past situations and had been my strength was no longer there. I was in a desert place. There was no song. I wallowed in despair, and deep down yearned in my spirit for restoration, and assurance that God was in control-recalling how in years gone past whatever I was going through, I still had this unshakable faith that the answer would come and that deliverance was on the way.

By now I had stopped praying and questioned if God even heard or indeed cared. My daughter's health was a very big concern. It was complicated, and her condition was getting to a desperate level. I looked on helplessly as she worsened, and wrote several letters to doctors and specialist to do something before it was too late. Nothing seemed to

work, and my daughter became more isolated and sick. Added to this there were issues with my own health, and the church I attended simply turned its back on us, and I desperately tried to understand why they were so cold and uncaring.

My husband was hurting as much as me, and we sank deeper into despair going over the problems again and again. In fact we had many 'pity parties together.'

In this state of helplessness it was impossible to be an encouragement, so we could not give any spiritual encouragement to our daughter or her family as we were empty ourselves.

I had certainly no desire to forgive anyone who wronged me, and my heart became cold and unyielding. I barely recognised myself. But God, in His grace and mercy had the plan of recovery well in place!

For about two weeks I had an inner prompting to attend the 'African Church' in Elgin. I knew nothing about it, and wondered why this thought kept coming to my mind. I was hesitant to even mention it to my husband as it seemed so ridiculous, but eventually did, and he agreed we should go.

Nothing could have prepared us for what lay in store. As soon as we entered we were greeted with warmth that was so genuine it touched our hearts. It was amazing; God's love was embracing us through these wonderful people who demonstrated a joy, a heavenly JOY! We felt like royalty! And the Pastor's name too was JOY (AYO). It was like finding precious stones, and as we attended week by week God began to pour His love into the damaged parts of our lives.

One particular sermon stands out as the Pastor preached on God providing a way of escape, and I realised that the doubts and fears I had carried for so long were worthless baggage, and I had no need of them. Jesus said: My yoke is easy and MY burden is light.

Grace and mercy had to become my companions, and I found it wasn't a struggle for me anymore to forgive and to release the hurts to God, who had been waiting patiently for me all this time.

As we had now been attending for several weeks, I began to share with the Pastor my concerns about my daughter's ill health, and consequently he asked if it would be possible to pray with her as God laid it on his heart to pray and fast for her healing. Caroline agreed, and the pastor and Ade visited her home. They shared communion together, prayed anointed her with oil, and commanded the sickness to go in Jesus name. From that day the depression has gone! Praise the Lord.

The evidence is clear for all to see, and has provided wonderful opportunities to tell of the miracle that has changed Caroline's life and touched so many others as she told them of what God has done. It is evident!

I thank God for His wonderful provision, and marvel at how much He loves us all. It amazes me that He desires to perfect His plan for our lives, and that He never gives up on us.

God heard and miraculously answered the faltering and my sometimes doubting prayer. No one but God could have arranged for a Nigerian Pastor, living in Aberdeen, and travelling to Elgin every Sunday in obedience to His call to be the instrument for this miracle.

I pray that this testimony will encourage anyone who is experiencing difficulties in their lives at this time to take courage; God is on your side. He knows you by name, and He knows your circumstances, but more importantly He has the answer to all your problems. Trust Him, praise Him. You may be tempted to give up, but He will never give up on you.

Thank you Lord for your mercy which far exceeds your judgement! Thank you for your grace which is limitless and free! Thank you for your great love which is unconditional. You are the source of joy, the giver, the deliverer, the healer, and you remain faithful from generation to generation. Praise your name!

SECRETS FROM GOD'S CONSTRUCTION SITE

Prayer, the power-house of the church, has allowed the Church to reap the immense benefits of God's faithfulness. The secrets of prayers as we understand include:

Prayer is a weapon for warfare

Prayer is a medium for communicating with God our Father. No doubt, in the course of the work in Jesus House it has become clear that, indeed, prayer is the key to breakthroughs. God is interested in our prayers and our prayers open doors and makes ways in the midst of life's dark alleys.

It can and will always fix things for us. This is because God always answers prayers and all we are required to do is tell our challenges to Him and wait for His reply. We have full assurance in this process in line with Christ's instruction:

"Ask, and it shall be given you; seek, and ye shall find; knock and it shall be opened unto you:

For every one that asketh receiveth; and he that seeketh findeth; and to him that knocketh it shall be opened. Or what man is there of you, whom if his son ask bread, will he give him a stone? Or if he ask a fish, will he give him a serpent? If ye then, being evil, know how to give good gifts unto your children, how much more shall your Father which is in heaven give good things to them that ask him? – Matthew 7. 7-11 (KJV)

Our God is a good and just God and would not give us what would not be good for us. The only thing He needs us to do is to ask Him.

Another reason why we see prayer as the key to our breakthrough is premised on the statement Jesus Christ made while explaining why His disciples could not cast out the demon from a young boy. He said:

This kind can come forth noth-

ing, but by prayer and fasting. Mark 9.29b (KJV)

God expects us to pray to have a breakthrough. Hence in difficult and hard times, there is a need to pray and fast until we break through with victory.

God's heart can be touched in the place of prayer

If my people, which are called by my name, shall humble themselves, and pray, and seek my face, and turn from their wicked ways; then will I hear from heaven, and will forgive their sins, and will heal their land. 2 Chronicles 7.14 (KJV)

Our prayers move God to act on our behalf. All he needs from us is to humble ourselves and pray and he will heal and perfect all that concerns us.

Our prayers are essential for God to act on our behalf. Let us therefore keep on in the spirit of prayers and the Righteous One will intervene on our behalf

PRAYER WALK 2007

Pastor Mark and Segun ministering to someone during the prayer walk

Jesus House folks praying at Castle Gate in Aberdeen

Chapter 6

CHURCH WITHOUT WALLS
TOUCHING PEOPLE,
ONE LIFE AT A TIME

The subject of love has been spoken of and professed by many, yet, what we see in the world today are actually manifestations of lust and self centeredness. Sadly, this trend has gradually crept into the church of God as a whole. At Jesus House Aberdeen, we aim to share God's love with all and sundry based on biblically-rooted principles. You may wonder what God's own standard for love is. This is the love that is patient, kind, not envious, and neither boastful nor proud.

Love does not dishonour others; not self-seeking, not easily angered, keeps no record of wrong, does not delight in evil but rejoices with the truth, always protects, always trusts, always hopes, and always preserves (1Cor. 13). As a people in Jesus House, this forms the basis for the Love we profess and which we practice.

Love is intertwined in our story, our history, our passion and our future. We are not perfect but day after day, we work to maintain love as our focus and, therefore, aim to reach out to the unsaved with the good news of our Lord Jesus Christ.

Love has proved a vital tool utilised by the church to ensure the growth and expansion of the Missions work in Aberdeen and Europe as a whole. At inception, the Lord blessed the church with one of such instruments for propagating His love, Mummy Akinmoladun. She was indeed a mother to many as highlighted in a previous chapter of this work. To the Glory of God, through her, a lot of people came to be members of the church, became committed and dedicated for the Master's use.

Another instrument in the propagation of God's Agape Love, especially through such means as discipleship and follow-up, was Pastor Mark Igiehon and his wife Alero Igiehon. Choosing the path of selfless-living, they were always there for the congregation to support and extend the right hand of fellowship. In the early days, for example, Pastor Mark drove round the city picking up members for service and at the end of the service dropped them off at their different homes; this was his routine every Sunday. Pastor Mark and his wife also fell into the habit of inviting people for lunch, dinner and day-outs.

Also worthy of mention are Femi Akarakiri and his wife Nneka. Caring was ingrained in their very nature. Reaching out in love, they had most youths, who they offered godly counsel and encouragements, swirling around them. Similarly, they invited the youths and whole departments most weekends in the summer to their home for barbeques, lunch and get-togethers.

BBQ at Femi Akarakiri's: Femi congratulates winner of dance contest- Helen Omole

The early church had weekly meetings on neutral non threatening grounds every Thursday at the Tiger-Tiger Bar, Aberdeen. The meeting was aimed at reaching out to people who ordinarily would not come to church. Here, people met with the pastor and discussed various life challenges in the midst of light refreshments. These meetings were power-packed and, not only were there restorations to ailing relationships; many believers were brought into the Kingdom. The question of our choice of a pub for the venue of the meetings is perhaps, best addressed by Paul's assertion:

Tobi Ojuile and Segu Akinkugbe dancing at a Barbeque party

"For though I be free from all men, yet have I made myself servant unto all, that I might gain the more. And unto the Jews I became as a Jew, that I might gain the Jews; to them that are under the law, as under the law, that I might gain them that are under the law; To them that are without law, as without law, (being not with-

out law to God, but under the law to Christ,) that I might gain them that are without law. To the weak became I as weak, that I might gain the weak: I am made all things to all men that I might by all means save some."1 Corinthians 9.19 - 22 (KJV)

TIGER-TIGER MEETINGS:
Thursday Good Life fellowship at Bar ICI

The church had the mindset that everyone deserves a chance to hear the truth of the gospel one way or the other. All these were done so as to influence the lives of people positively and in the process, gain some for Christ. From Tiger-Tiger, the church moved the fellowship to Archibald Simpson and then to Bar ICI. All these meetings were aimed at reaching out to many.

These great minds did this faithfully and the Lord indeed has rewarded their labour of love. The church has grown so much through this care and support. To the Glory of God Pastor Mark Igiehon is determined to raise mighty men for the Kingdom

just as David did during his days. Taking people who would have been otherwise considered to be of no value, investing in them and following them up to the point where they became fit for the Master's use.

As the church grew, this fellowship evolved to house fellowships, in different parts of the city. With the mandate to reach out to the different neighbourhoods in the city, the fellowships are founded church members. Thus, giving them an opportunity to socialize, get to know one another, build friendships, study the Bible and pray together. These fellowships were instituted following the biblical example of the brethren at the Philadelphia church who were known for the love they had for each other, their unity of purpose and oneness of mind.

The church today has so grown that a unit, the Welcome and Follow-up Department, that specifically takes care of caring, follow-up and welfare of the members of the church has been set up, with the aim of ensuring discipleship of members.

THE LAZARUS MINISTRY

Apart from caring and reaching out to members of the body of Christ, the church, in recent times, has devised different strategies for caring for the local community. One of such arm through which the church is achieving this goal is the Lazarus Ministry. This group operates fully on the streets of Aberdeen every Friday night. They serve as street angels; ministering and praying with drug addicts, alcoholics and people in need. Through this outreach they minister Jesus Christ and encourage the lost and perishing to give their lives to Jesus so they can be made whole and delivered from all forms of addiction and depression. This ministry is led by Sis Agnes Tandi.

JESUS HOUSE – COME ALONG FOR SOME FUN!

In the thick of serious kingdom business, the Jesus House Church ensures that there's room for informal interactions and loads of fun. Contrary to popular perception of the church as a place characterised

Hill Climbing Event - Getting to the top felt sweet as Pastor Mark and Ogechi take a quick rest

Members dancing at Pastor Mark's birthday dinner party, 2007

JH Football team

by boredom, we believe that church is fun and several non-traditional church activities are organised to drive home that point. One avenue is the sports groups. There is a football team and also an annual hill-climbing exercise organised with the aim of allowing members to exercise and have fun at the same time. These activities are organised by the men's fellowship.

Furthermore a time-out is organised annually and may be in form of a trip, a barbeque party, a picnic, an indoor game (like bowling) or a beach party. These events hold mainly during the summer and have, so far been successful.

Children were not left out at a
JH barbeque party 2009

Some
Participants
of the
Bus tour

Habiba,
Tope and
Izu at Gala
night 2011

REACHING OUT TO OUR WORLD

Jesus House Aberdeen is also actively involved in reaching out to her community. One of such is the "God's Abode in Elderly People's Home (GAIEPH)". This outreach focuses on reaching out to the elderly people in the community and this is done in form of carols and visitations at various elderly homes in Aberdeen.

This initiative was pioneered by Eunice Adesina.

Church members at a barbeque

Another of such is the outreaches held at festive periods including Easter and Christmas. This outreach is aimed at reaching out to different communities in the city at these times of the year; sharing in love with them the reason for the season. In the course of these outreaches, welfare packs containing food and clothing are given to those who need or want them in such localities.

TESTIMONY REPORTS

MIRACLES DO HAPPEN
– MARVIS AMADI

They say miracles do happen, I agree as I am not just an observer but a privileged partaker of a miracle. *My daughter, are you still crying?* What did you say I mumbled in the midst of tears? My mum replied *"I said go to the altar, lie down there with*

Roland, Marvis and their baby

the doctors report and see if the most high God who reigns in the affairs of men would not turn your situation around".

That was my mother's counsel over the phone, a simple instruction. It kept ringing in my head just as much as the weight of the doctor's report I had just received. *"We are sorry to give you this upsetting news but due to the extent of the damage done your chance of ever having a baby is slim".*

There were so many questions on my mind - What had I done to get into this situation? What had gone wrong? Where were my dreams and hopes barely few months after getting married? A little carelessness on my part and an irreparable damage had resulted. I took some medications in the first few weeks of pregnancy, un-prescribed drugs a means of self medication but the result was the loss of the pregnancy and perforations in the womb.

Labeled as barren, this information was too much for me to bear hence the call to my mother. As instructed by my mum I went to church, looking left then right no one seemed to notice. I approached the altar with trepidation wondering to myself what I was doing here for at that very moment I had been booked for an appointment with a counselor to review my options for adoption.

I laid upon the altar of God at the City of God and wept and this became my routine for a whole week. Time went by, days turned into weeks and then I discovered something had happened. It was too good to be true, could it be possible? I checked the test result again and it was positive. I was pregnant!

I reported the new development to my doctor. Initially, she found it hard to believe but after a series of confirmatory tests it was established that indeed something rare had occurred and I had conceived. Month after month the pregnancy progressed under the close scrutiny of medical staff and finally it was 9 months.

Preparations were in full swing for the birth of this miracle child then, something seemed to have gone wrong because the baby wasn't forthcoming. I had gone beyond 40 weeks and still no sign of labour. But as the bible says in His time He makes all things beautiful. On the 3rd of January after quite a prolonged labour I delivered a beautiful baby girl, Adrial Oroma. Everyone was excited and relieved that it was finally over or so we thought.

A day after delivery I discovered my baby was not breathing, I shouted out for help and the nurses and medics came to my aid. Like a dream she was rushed into intensive care and the battle for her life began. Apparently due to the prolonged labour she had passed her first bowel motion (meconium) in the womb and this had gotten into her lungs and blocked it. Unfortunately it was not noticed at delivery so it gradually affected her breathing until it got to a critical stage.

Three agonizing weeks went by and the condition did not seem to improve but the church kept praying, various ministers kept a prayer vigil believing God for a turn around. God heard the prayers and a turnaround did come and we were eventually discharged by the specialist.

My daughter is a testimony that indeed with "With man some things may be impossible, but with God all things are possible."

Pastor Mark with Ministers at Peniel 2009 barbeque party

Buses at a tourist site 2006

Bus tour participants with tour guides during the Bus tour

Izu and Pastor Jide at Awards night 2011

SECRETS FROM GOD'S CONSTRUCTION SITE

The Children of a loving God must love unconditionally

God loves us unconditionally and he wants us to love those around us in the same manner as he loved us; irrespective of background, colour, race or circular circumstances and should not matter when we reach out to others.

Fill up and complete my joy by living in harmony and being of the same mind and one in purpose, having the same love, being in full accord and of one harmonious mind and intention. Do nothing from factional motives [through contentiousness, strife, selfishness, or for unworthy ends] or prompted by conceit and empty arrogance.

Instead, in the true spirit of humility (lowliness of mind) let each regard the others as better than and superior to himself [thinking more highly of one another than you do of yourselves]. Let each of you esteem and look upon and be concerned for not [merely] his own interests, but also each for the interests of others.

Let this same attitude and purpose and [humble] mind be in you which

was in Christ Jesus: [Let Him be your example in humility:] – Philippians 2. 2-5 (Amplified)

Apostle Paul, here, admonishes the church at Philippi to have the same mind that was in Christ. Jesus Christ loved unconditionally and expects us to love one another as ourselves. It is a command: *"Thou shalt not avenge, nor bear any grudge against the children of thy people, but thou shalt love thy neighbour as thyself: I am the LORD. – Leviticus 19.18(KJV)"* This attitude and mind is what God expects of us.

Over the years, we have learnt that no matter what we do, if we do not love God or the people around us, our labour will be in vain (1 Corinthians 13). Love conquers all and covers all sins. Hence, we are encouraged to love all in our thoughts, words and actions.

God wants us to reach out to the unreached

It is God's heart-desire to have us reach the unreached by preaching to those who are yet to know about the Lord Jesus.

"...not willing that any should perish, but that all should come to repentance." – 2 Peter 3.9b (KJV)

God's desire is that no one should perish but come to the full knowledge of the saving grace of God and therefore come to repentance. Repentance comes after godly sorrow for our sins, leading to salvation in Jesus Christ; with a firm decision not to go back to our sinful ways. Since it is God's desire, then He expects us who know him to share the good news with others so that others can benefit from our testimonies.

Hence, as individuals we are encouraged to ensure that our actions and lifestyle reflect the life of God so that others can see it and want to be a part of God's family. Reaching out means loving and love is God.

There is strength in unity

We are aware that there is strength in unity and are convinced that love, care and fellowship increases the love members have for each other. Hence, the brethren are encouraged to work together to achieve great things.

And the whole earth was of one language, and of one speech. And it came to pass, as the journeyed from the east that they found a plain in the land of Shinar; and they dwelt there. And they said one to another, Go to, let us make brick, and burn them thoroughly. And they had brick for stone, and slime had they for morter. And they said, Go to, let us build us a city and a tower, whose top may reach unto heaven; and let us make us a name, lest we be scattered abroad upon the face of the whole earth.

And the LORD came down to see the city and the tower, which the children of men builded. And the LORD said, Behold, the people is one, and they have all one language; and this they begin to do: and now nothing will be restrained from them, which they have imagined to do.

– Genesis 11.1-6

From the story of the tower of Babel, we see that because the people were one, there was nothing that they imagined that they could not do. This applies to us as well. In all things, we strive to work with one mind because unity determines how far we can go as a people and as a group.

Chapter 7

HELP FROM ABOVE

I look up to the mountains— does my help come from there? My help comes from the Lord, who made heaven and earth!

— Psalm 121.1 (NLT)

God is our refuge and strength, a very present help in trouble.

— Psalm 46.1 (KJV)

Here, the Psalmist speaks of the source of his strength, the Lord. The Lord is his refuge, strength and ever present help in times of trouble (need). As a church, we say this is our testimony. The Lord has always been and still is our help as a church. He has indeed sent us helpers.

Through the years, Jesus House has been favoured of God who has sent divine helpers for the furtherance of the business of the kingdom. In the early days, the Lord used Hazel McAllan the lady in charge of the Bal-

nagask community centre to bless the church. Hazel was selfless in her help and introduced the church to different things that would benefit her. Through her was the church invited to the Torry Gala that holds annually. And through the Gala, the presence of the church was felt in the community. Hazel has been supportive, helpful to the church and easy to reach both at home. She gave the church easy access to her heart and was used tremendously by God.

Jesus House Celebrates Hazel on her Birthday

THE SCOTTISH GOVERNMENT MEETS OUR GOD

Another person that the Lord has used in a tremendous fashion in the work of the church is Alan Donnelly; Councillor for the Torry and Ferryhill constituencies in Aberdeen at the time of this work. Our first encounter with him was during the open day held on the 12th of March 2009 to present the City of God Building to the civic and political leadership of Aberdeen, which had the crème of Aberdonian politics in atten-

LORD PROVOST AT OPEN DAY

Special Guests at Open Day
@City of God

dance including the Lord Provost. After that event, Alan Donnelly has been a tremendous support of the church and has attended subsequent programs of the church including Battle of the Bands, Aberdeen Mass Choir Concert, and Christmas party/ carol services. During the 2010 election, he was involved in the Churches arrangement with MP candidates to share their manifesto to the members of the church. These events have become outstanding evangelistic avenues for attracting locals to church, giving them the opportunity to hear the good news.

THE CHURCH AND THE GOVERNMENT

A school of thought opines that the business of the church is totally different from the matter of the state or government and both function differently. The logical reasoning behind that saying notwithstanding, we understand from the scriptures that they actually go hand in hand. God has called us as kings and priests to him. Hence, we can function in both offices. In order to ensure that we play our roles effectively in our world, the Bible instructs Christians to pray for the rulers of the land to make the right decisions at the right time.

In recent times, Jesus House has delegated representatives to work with Pastor John Holmes (the Flying pastor) on an outreach known as Operation Great Britain. The team attend the different meetings and suggest God's own idea of how different matters of the state should be addressed as well as praying for the leadership of the land. This group is known as Operation Great Britain. This way, we give back to the people and the government through our prayers and fellowship with them.

We hope, therefore, that order would be reinstated and that Aberdeen would return to her first love. This group is coordinated by Joe Ochie. Although the ministry has just commenced work, we pray and believe that through this ministry, the voice of the church would be heard once more in the land and the people would be drawn back to God.

SECRETS FROM GOD'S CONSTRUCTION SITE

God can use anyone

But God hath chosen the foolish things of the world to confound the wise; and God hath chosen the weak things of the world to confound the things which are mighty.
1 Corinthians 1.27 (KJV)

One of the things we have learnt is that God can use anyone He chooses to, even the people we least expect Him to use. The people considered as unimportant are typically those God delights in using to bring forth great breakthroughs. We need to consider every opportunity God gives us as rare because He can use anyone He chooses. Hence, these opportunities should be treasured.

God has an enormous army

God has a large army beyond our imagination. For every circumstance and phase His church would encounter, the Lord already has people prepared for such moves.

Let us not at anytime think that we can keep God on our waiting list, or put Him on hold till we feel we are ready to do what He wants us to do. He has people who would always do the things He wants to achieve in His church.

God has replacements.

Not only does God use anyone or a large army; He can replace anyone at anytime or moment. Every moment for service is an opportunity to give God our best. Once we decide that we are doing too much or make the rules for God, He quickly replaces us with people who are willing. This shows that no one is irreplaceable.

And they brought him to Jesus: and they cast their garments upon the colt, and they set Jesus thereon. And as he went, they spread their clothes in the way. And when he was come nigh, even now at the descent of the mount of Olives, the whole multitude of the disciples began to rejoice and praise God with a loud voice for all the mighty works that they had seen; Saying, Blessed be the King that cometh in the name of the Lord:

peace in heaven, and glory in the highest. And some of the Pharisees from among the multitude said unto him, Master, rebuke thy disciples. And he answered and said unto them, I tell you that, if these should hold their peace, the stones would immediately cry out. – Luke 19.35-40 (KJV)

This account records the opposition faced from the Pharisees by those who were jubilant and exalting Jesus during His entry into Jerusalem. They confronted Jesus, asking Him to stop His disciples from praising Him. In response, Jesus told them that everyone was replaceable because if they stopped praising Him, the stones will rise up to take their place. This clearly shows that we ought to be very careful to serve the Lord diligently at every point in time in the place of service.

EASTER OUTREACH AT TILLYDRONE 2010

Chapter 8

MENDING BROKEN WALLS:

THE NEHEMIAH GENERATION

In 2007, the Lord indicated through Pastor Mark Igiehon that it was going to be 'the year of Nehemiah' for the church. The year was to be dedicated to rebuilding the broken walls of individual lives as well as re-establishing the Kingdom of God in Aberdeen. It was a year that Jesus House Aberdeen prayed for the revival of the church in Scotland as well as the rebuilding of her broken walls.

As a result, an intensive study of the book of Nehemiah was undertaken and priority given to rebuilding of lives and relationships as well as the re-enactment of a praying culture.

THE QUEST FOR GOD'S TABERNACLE

As the church grew, the Balnagask Community Centre increasingly became inadequate to cater for the growing number of God's children. Consequently, the church set out to look for a permanent, bigger tabernacle. The church interest for different church buildings listed on the building market which (at the time) was typically on sale for conversion into pubs, casinos, night clubs, block of flats or offices; desecrating the house of God.

The first bid was for a church building at Mid-Stocket road but we were unsuccessful. However, we prayed and handed the build-

CITY OF GOD BUILDING

CITY OF GOD BUILDING

A section of members dancing for joy during the inauguration of Jesus House at City of God

City of God Altar in Auditorium before renovation

A section of the church before renovation

Pastor Kola Bolanta at the chapel before renovation

DADDY GO AT THE DEDICATION OF CITY OF GOD BUILDING

Pastor Mark takes Daddy GO and other ministers on a tour round the building

Daddy GO dedicates the Building to God

Pastor Mark and Joe Ochie with Pastor Enoch Adeboye and Pastor Agu Irukwu at the entrance of COG before the dedication of the building.

Provincial Pastor Kola Bolanta
delivering the message

Pastor Mark singing for joy at the
Inaugural Service

Arrival of new chairs for the City of God property

Onii Madu ministering at the Inaugural service

ing to the Most High confident that going forward, God's property would be left consecrated for Him.

As a church, we did not lose hope, because we knew the Lord had something greater in store for us. In March 2007, we put in another bid for the then Holburn Central Church, Church of Scotland; and the Lord miraculously gave us success over and above eighteen other interested groups. To God's glory, the building was redeemed from being converted to another pub, casino, night club, block of flats or offices. Then, it dawned on us that 2007 was indeed a year to redeem, rebuild and reclaim for the Lord. As a church we are still running with the mandate of possessing the land for the Lord. After the bid was won, we started to raise funds for it and to the Glory of God we were able to acquire the building.

On 2nd of December 2007 the church moved into the building and had her inaugural service at the building.

VISION FOR GOD'S HOUSE (1 CHRON 22.5)

And David said, Solomon my son is young and tender, and the house that is to be builded for the LORD must be exceeding magnifical, of fame and of glory throughout all countries: I will therefore now make preparation for it. So David prepared abundantly before his death. – 1Chronicles 22.5 (KJV)

On acquiring the building work on its renovation commenced in full swing to make it a befitting place of worship. To the Glory of God the first and second phases of the restructuring have been successfully completed. God has really made His house famous indeed as it has adorned the pages of the Press and Journal newspaper Aberdeen as well as the Sunrise Magazine. It has also hosted dignitaries; the church had the honour to host the Lord Provost of Aberdeen on 14th of March, 2010.

OPEN DAY REPORT
BY ANULI DIGWO

"A message of joy going out to the world" – Lord Provost of Aberdeen describing Jesus House Aberdeen's mission

Jesus House @ City of God held its Open Day on Saturday 14th March 2009. This was an initiative to unveil the church and its building to the people of Aberdeen and its environs, and in particular, members of the Church of Scotland from whom we inherited the church building. In attendance were the political leaders of Aberdeen: The Lord Provost (civic head of Aberdeen), Peter Stephen, councillors Kirsty West of Hilton/Stockethill constituency and Allan Donnelly of Torry/Ferryhill constituency, Deputy Provost, John West ably represented by his P.A. Members of the former Holburn Central parish church [prior to sale of building to Jesus House] were in attendance led by Rev. George Cowie (then minister of the parish, now minister of South Holburn Church).

The event kicked off with a welcome speech by Pastor Mark Igiehon, in which he outlined the mission statement of the church and the fact that it is a community of all nations open to all, despite having its origins in Nigeria. The Lord Provost in his speech expressed delight at the children's presentation, commending the blend of nice music, smiling faces and happiness radiated. He noted that in this era when churches face stagnation, and church buildings are being converted into pubs and night clubs, it comes as a wonderful revelation to see the growth of Jesus House Aberdeen, and her vision in setting up sister parishes in Edinburgh, Dyce, Torry, Glasgow and other locations.

Rev. Cowie gave some insights on the history of the church and its building and expressed joy that the building was able to remain a place of worship. He reminisced that the building has a long standing relationship with the Gordon Highlanders (an Army Unit). Many years ago people stood in the city centre to watch the soldiers march down to the church for Sunday services. The stained windows upstairs were gifted by the Gordon Highlanders in memory of the deceased soldiers that partook in the South African campaign (early 1900s) and has the inscription "rejoice for God hath given us the city". This inscription interestingly coincides with the revelation given to our Church [Jesus House Aberdeen] in 2004 for a building to be called the "City of God". The event was well attended, and everyone attested to having had a wonderful time.

Smithfield Property: City of God Campus

The following is an excerpt describing the significance of Jesus House Aberdeen from his remarks at the Open Day event organised by the Church: *"A message of joy going out to the world" – Lord Provost of Aberdeen, Peter Stephen*

Not only did the church host the Lord Provost of Aberdeen, also in attendance at the event were the councillors Kirsty West representing the West of Hilton/Stockethill constituency, and Allan Donnelly of Torry/Ferryhill constituency. The Deputy Provost John West was represented by his Personal Assistant at the open day. Also present were the members of the former Holburn Central parish church led by former minister of the parish (and now minister of South Holburn Church) Rev. George Cowie.

The project has continued to the glory of God and the Lord has spread His fame abroad through this building. Thankfully, the acquisition of the church building marked the end of the trend of conversion of church buildings into pubs. It has also given us a testimony that other churches have been encouraged by.

While still revelling in God's provision, He blessed us with yet another beautiful building. Recently the Lord helped us redeem the former St John's Church for the Deaf Smithfield, Aberdeen. On this occasion, we were approached to buy the property by the Aberdeen and North East Deaf Society managing the building lost their support from the City Council. To the praise of our God, the building is now known as the City of God Campus and the church within it is the City of the Great King.

TESTIMONY REPORT

HISTORY OF HOLBURN CENTRAL CHURCH NOW CITY OF GOD

BY UCHECHI UCHE DIBIAEZUE

The people of Aberdeen have always had a thirst for God. For example, due to the pressing need for more places of worship consequent upon population growth, in 1835, a meeting was held, where it was decided that a Church be built near Justice Mills on Union Street. Voluntary contributions were made to provide cheap sitting for the poor, and the church which commenced service in 1836 was known as The Holburn church.

This new church was not very successful; resulting in the resignation of its first preacher Mr. James Leslie and the appointment of a new one, the Rev. William T. Mitchell. In those days, church attendees were known to pay for a certain number of pews (seats) for the exclusive use of members of their family during church services; a practice that was regarded as a heritable privilege and one held in high esteem.

Unprecedented Growth

Dr. McClymont was one minister who made a difference in the 39years he spent as the minister of the Holburn church before he retired in 1912. Church membership grew from 900 to 1966 members and it became the 3rd largest parish of the Church of Scotland. Extensive improvements were made in the church: a hall (1881) and tower (1891) were built to beautify the church; stained glass windows and electric lights were put in, and he personally bought the church bell.

He assigned three districts within Aberdeen: Hardgate, College Street and Ruthrieston for mission service, spreading the gospel to these parts. A memorial tablet in honour of Dr McClymont's contributions still hangs in the church today. The increase in membership continued and resulted in the establishment of some mission churches such as the Ruthrieston as separate parishes. Furthermore, new

UCHECHI UCHE

parishes were built at Rubislaw and Mannorfield in order to draw imaginary boundaries for the Holburn church, but it rather grew in membership reaching a massive 4000.

In 1925, the name of the church was changed from Holburn Church to Holburn Central Parish. The church continued to grow in membership and in its influence on the community. One of its ministers, Dr. Knox who became the minister of the church in 1961 went to Nigeria in 1974 to become the director of one of its theological schools dedicated to the training of the ministers of God. The church also held services for the soldiers of the Gordon Highlanders, and became known as "Sojers kirk" (garrison church), especially during the tenure of Rev. Ian Scott, who was the minister from 1975 – 1982.

A New Chapter

When Rev. Ian Scott was minister at the church, he raised some concerns over the decline in Church attendance, particularly among the young people. As the town of Aberdeen grew, a lot of Church members moved away from the city centre to the suburbs. City growth also came with many distractions as shops were now open on Sunday mornings, and recreational activities for children such as football practices held on Sundays.

It became difficult to get the youths interested in church and over the years, the average age of churchgoers has averaged the 60 years mark. Deaths also contributed to the membership decline. Aberdeen Presbytery under the Church of Scotland constituted a committee to review its churches and their viability for continued existence, and the Holburn Central church was one of the churches that was put up for evaluation. The committee studied the Holburn Central church over a futuristic 10 year span and came to the conclusion that it would be out of use due to declining membership. The Holburn Central church was therefore merged with Ruthrieston; one of its mission churches.

The Holburn Central church building, located at the centre of Aberdeen city, made it a prime choice for developers and was put up for sale with bids coming from different organizations; each with various ideas of what they wanted to use the church building for including proposals for its use as a pubs, restaurants, shops, or apartment building. The Redeemed Christian Church of God, Jesus House Parish successfully won the bid, which meant that the church would continue to be used as a place of worship and service to God. The Church of God is marching on, and the gates of hell shall not prevail against it (Matthew 16:18) in Jesus' name.

Easter Outreach at Bridge of Don 2011

**Article from The Press and Journal Aberdeen on Saturday29 December, 2007.
Title: City Church is bought by Christian group (Andrew Hamilton)**

Saturday December 29 2007
www.thisisnorthscotland.co.uk

The Press and Journal
NEWS ABERDEEN

City church is bought by Christian group

KIRK TO REMAIN A HOUSE OF GOD DESPITE PROPERTY DEVELOPMENT FEARS

BY ANDREW HAMILTON

WHEN it was put on to the property market, many feared Aberdeen's Holburn Central Church would be the latest place of worship to be transformed into a bar or flats. However, a Christian group has intervened to ensure that the church will remain a house of God.

The B-listed church and hall were first advertised late last year as "suitable for conversion into residential units, or for leisure or business use", with offers of more than £450,000 invited.

Despite reported interest from commercial bodies looking to convert the Holburn Street building, the successful bidder was Jesus House Aberdeen, a branch of the Redeemed Christian Church of God (RCCG).

According to its website, Jesus House Aberdeen saw off challenges from 19 developers, and expressed confidence in raising the purchase price of £1.1million.

A statement on the organisation's website said: "Visiting Aberdeen, you will see magnificent church buildings now turned to pubs, casinos, nightclubs and restaurants.

"But we thank the Lord because the magnificent former Holburn West Church of Scotland, right in Aberdeen's city centre, will remain as a place of worship."

RCCG is a full gospel, Bible-believing, Pentecostal worldwide church. There are more than 340 RCCG churches in the UK and Ireland, with 12 in Scotland and three in Aberdeen.

The other RCCG churches in the city are at Palmerston Road and Balnagask Road.

A Church of Scotland spokeswoman confirmed that Jesus House Aberdeen had successfully bid for the church earlier this month.

SAVED: Aberdeen's Holburn Central Church will remain as a kirk. Photograph: Jim Irvine

Article from Sunrise titled:City of God risein Aberdeen

...ure from The SUNRISE Magazine, the official publication of the RCCG Central Office

TESTIMONIES

CITY OF GOD RISES IN ABERDEEN

The miracle of how Jesus House Aberdeen's Project Nehemiah reclaimed a foothold for Christ in the heart of the City.

By Femi Akarakiri and Idongesit Umoh

At the end of Oscar road in Torry, Aberdeen is the Torry Community Sports Centre. Here, on June 6th, 2004, six people gathered at its basketball court to hold the very first service of Jesus House Aberdeen, a parish of the Redeemed Christian Church of God (RCCG), planted by Jesus House Port Harcourt. By September 2004, we had moved to the Balnagask Community Centre in Torry. We witnessed the mighty hand of God in increasing membership to the extent that the Balnagask Community Center was no longer capable of accommodating the needs of the growing church.

Churches to Pubs

Concerns have been raised by visiting men of God in recent times over the conversion of Aberdeen Church buildings into alternative secular uses: as offices, residential flats and worse still, pubs and clubs. Prayers have been offered in front of many of these desecrated church buildings for their reversion to their original use, and that no other church buildings should suffer the same fate.

The Prophecy: Project Nehemiah

In January, 2007, God through His servant, Pastor Mark Igiehon of Jesus House Aberdeen prophetically declared the year as "The Year of Nehemiah". The biblical book of Nehemiah details the Project undertaken by Nehemiah and the people of Judah in rebuilding the city of Jerusalem, its walls and gates. In the same light, Project Nehemiah challenged us to take back what belongs to the Lord in our City of Aberdeen; rebuild the altar of God in the city once again; get a befitting Church property of "our" own, and build up our individual and collective spiritual lives for greater responsibilities in the Kingdom.

Seeking the Sanctuary

Our initial bid for a disused church building on Aberdeen's Midstocket Road met with disappointment, but God does not see as men see; little did we know then that He was not interested in relocating us from one hidden place in the city to another one. Rather, He sees His Church as a city set upon the hill that cannot and should not be hidden.

Shortly after this, we noted that the Holburn Central Parish building would be up for sale. This church is right in the heart of the city, at the beginning of Union Street, the main artery of Aberdeen life. The building was put up for sale by the Church of Scotland (CoS) by sealed bids. 19 companies with various interests came forward with proposals to convert the building to pubs, restaurants, shopping and other purposes. Jesus House was the only interest from a Church and the only bid to continue using the building as God's house. Having considered all things, an amount of £1.1 million was inspired by the Lord as the bid amount. Thanks be to God who had ordained that the Holburn building would remain an altar to His Name forever. To our own joyful surprise, we were informed of the success of our bid against those of others. This was a joyous moment in the JH congregation with thanksgiving to God that the altar would not be desecrated. The next challenge was to raise the funds.

THE REDEEMED CHRISTIAN CHURCH OF GOD

Nehemiah Project Coordinator, Femi and Wife

Special song by the choir

Open Heaven

The entire Church called on the Name of our God to do that which only He could do in this situation. The huge amount meant that except God Himself did it, there was absolutely no way that amount could be raised. Raising this amount became an exercise in faith for the whole JH church. Cars were sold, houses re-mortgaged, equities and stocks sold. People worked extra hours, all to make money available to meet the £450k down-payment for a mortgage with the Royal Bank of Scotland. Members spent their time and resources to correspond with potential donors both within the UK and in other parts of the world.

We initially met with a lot of disappointment, and when all seemed dim, we went back to God in heartfelt prayers and He caused doors to open with huge contributions coming from Jesus House Port-Harcourt, and renewed commitment from the members. Donations were also received from friends, colleagues at work, our senior sister parish, Fountain of Love Church Aberdeen, and from many other RCCG Churches in UK and beyond, leading to a sudden surge in funds flowing in and a boon to our faith.

Mention must be made of the patience and flexibility of the selling party, The Church of Scotland. We must also mention that the local Royal Bank of Scotland considered their funding of this project, as close to being an act of faith, as this would be their biggest funding for a church organization. The Holy Spirit inspired and directed us at every turn: what to bid, how to bid, how to raise funds, choice of bankers, solicitor, planning consultant, architect, surveyor, financial consultant, etc. Looking at our numbers at the time, the task was insurmountable but the Lord led our pastor and entire Church on a wonderful journey to increase our faith for this great project.

Testimonies

This great miracle has changed the spiritual landscape in Aberdeen. The

wonderful news has been reported in newspapers and news websites; two other churches in Aberdeen have approached us for guidance on acquiring other disused church buildings; even the Church of Scotland, perhaps amazed by the miracle, requested for the names of our consultants, not knowing that our Consultant is the Holy Spirit. Our architect is now renovating a CoS church in Glasgow in a scheme similar to our winning bid. The lives of all who are part of Project Nehemiah has been touched with awesome miracles; many miraculously moved into their own properties; spiritual growth; career and business advancements, etc.

Inaugural Service at the City of God Centre

To the glory of God, on 29th November, 2007, nearly 10 months after the bid was won, the financial arrangements were completed. On the 2nd of December, 2007 the building hosted the inaugural Church service with the Provincial Pastor of RCCG Rivers 3, Pastor Kola Bolanta who oversees our mother church, Jesus House Port Harcourt, leading the service.

We are now progressively transforming the building into a place that meets the standard set out in I Chro 22.5b: '... and the house that is to be builded for the LORD must be exceeding magnifical, of fame and of glory ...'.

The entire *Project Nehemiah* has been a journey of faith and demonstration of the faithfulness of our God. God indeed showed that He will build His church and the gates of hell shall not prevail against it. It is also evident that God does not need a multitude to effect His plans; a few with willing hearts is all that God requires so that no man will take the glory due unto Him. The book of 1 Samuel 14:5b says that "there is no restraint to the LORD to save by many or by few".

Long before we moved into the building, we prophetically understood and announced that the building will be named the *City of God* centre. Little did

we know how prophetic that was. Entering the building, we saw that, written in one of the stained glass windows was this quote: 'Rejoice for God has given you the city' from the book of Joshua 6.16! Prophetic message indeed! Truly the Lord has given us the City, and now we begin to possess it.

Aberdeen, here comes the Lord your God into the midst of thee!

Appreciation

We return all the glory and adoration to the Lord. We thank our parents Jesus House Port Harcourt who are parents indeed! Their giving to Project Nehemiah was awesome. We thank Fountain of Love Aberdeen whose insight, counsel, and gifts were tremendous. We thank all the pastors and parishes across the UK and US who sent their 'bricks' for God's house. The Lord will remember you all for good!

Dr. Giwa-Osagie & Family from JH Inverness

The Surtees

Choir

Pastor Bolanta

Choreography from City of God Scotland

Off to lunch

The ushers

SEMINARS

May 17th — Trustees Awareness Seminar & Gift Aid Seminar
June 21st — Church Accountants procedure & Church cash flow management
July 19th — The Pastor and his Marriage / The Pastor as a patient
September 20th — Evangelism on another Level
October 18th — The Pastor as a Shepherd, leader and mentor
Money Counting Procedures
The Pastor purchasing a building
The Pastor and his Deacons

Dates are still tentative. Further announcements will be made upon confirmation.

THE REDEEMED CHRISTIAN CHURCH OF GOD

SECRETS FROM GOD'S CONSTRUCTION SITE

Never give up

One of the vital lessons we have learnt and are still understanding is that failure at something does not mean one should not try again. Someone once defined the word "FAIL" as First Attempt In Learning. Another defined "failure" as a means at which something cannot be achieved or obtained.

From both definitions we deduce that God does not want us to quit trying when we fail at something because when we fail, we only discover how something ought not to be done. It also means we should keep trying until we get a result. When we lost the first bid, we encouraged ourselves and kept on believing in God. We didn't relax but kept on looking for possible buildings to buy.

In relation to our lives, we need to keep on trying even when we have failed. Our God is a God of a second, third, fourth, (and so on)

chances. He does not give up on us, so we should not give up on ourselves. Rather, we should keep on doing our best and in due season God will reward our labour.

• God's view point differs from man's

The first church we bid for at Mid-Stocket is in a residential part of the city, a bit removed from the city centre. When we put in our first bid for the church, we believed that God had given it to us physically. We continued in prayers, possessing the place in the Spirit. As God would have it, we did not win the bid. People would have expected us to give up but we did not; convinced that God had the perfect plan. The place of worship that God later gave to us became the best we could ask for. It was in the heart of the city, well within reach from all parts of the city.

From this experience, it is evident that God does not see as man sees. He always has the perfect plan for us and would always bring us to the place of rest he has for planned for us only if we believe.

God wants the best for you

As God's children, therefore, let us always be ready to receive the best from the father because that is what He has in store for us.

God is Alpha and Omega

God has perfect knowledge of how things will turn out because He is the Alpha and Omega, the beginning and the end. He knows all about us and knows the end of everything we venture into. All we can do is align ourselves to His will for us in other to get a positive result at the end.

Faithfulness in little things opens the doors for great things

From the story of Jesus House Aberdeen, it is seen that God commits more to those who are faithful over little. When the church bought the former Holburn Central Church, the church continued to ascribe the praise to God for the building. In addition, the church's mandate was to run with the same mandate David gave to his son (1 Chronicles 22.5).

Because of faithfulness, the Lord committed the Smithfield property in the hands of the church. Therefore, we ought to be faithful in everything committed in our hands and God will commit more to us.

VALENTINE BALL 2008

Chapter 9

GREAT EXPOITS OF MIGHTY MEN

David therefore departed thence, and escaped to the cave Adullam: and when his brethren and all his father's house heard it, they went down thither to him. And every one that was in distress, and every one that was in debt, and every one that was discontented, gathered themselves unto him; and he became a captain over them: and there were with him about four hundred men. And David went thence to Mizpeh of Moab: and he said unto the king of Moab, Let my father and my mother, I pray thee, come forth, and be with you, till I know what God will do for me. - 1 Samuel 22.1-3 (KJV)

In the above scripture, we see that David, while running away from King Saul, had men who were affiliated to him; people he could call on and depend upon at every point in time. These men were men people considered as non-influential in those days. In the later part in 2 Samuel 23, we see the exploits they did, unimaginable things that people would never have expected them to do. Just like in the days of David, the Lord has raised in Jesus House Aberdeen, mighty men and women to himself: men of valour, of zeal and courage, all to His Glory.

One of such men is **Femi Akarakiri.** Femi was fearless, bold and with much zeal. He was the first to see the City of God building and viewed the place before the church put in the bid. He took this as his own business and worked relentlessly to see that the church was successful in everything regarding the acquisition of the building. When the building was bought, he became the project coordinator and saw to it that the building was befitting for worship.

Not only did he handle the project Nehemiah, he was also involved in Sunday school.

Another man of like passion is **Dapo Otunla.** He stepped into the shoes of Femi and coordinated the completion of Project Nehemiah Phase two. Selfless in his service, he ensured the sign post of the church was sorted. Though a difficult task with the regulations involved in Scotland, he went on with it, fearless and

Using his talents and resources, he did most of the electrical wiring, fixed the projectors, bracketed unsightly pipes around the building, and did most of the interior painting. On completion of phase one of project Nehemiah which involved buying the building and making it habitable, he proceeded to the second phase of the project where he coordinated the carpeting of the building, setting up of the church office and bookshop, erecting of the podium for the technical team and acquisition of befitting chairs to make the place magnificent. All these he did to the Glory of God until his relocation to Nigeria in 2008.

tackling every challenge that came in the approval process. He equally coordinated the addition of more offices and meeting rooms in the City of God. All these he did

fully until he returned to Nigeria for a short while, leaving the church to Segun Akinkugbe's care and was later joined by Emmanuel Omuederiaye. On his return from Nigeria in 2008, he went on another mission; this time to support the work at Edinburgh started Iyalla Ibiyekariwaripiribo until his final return to Nigeria in December, 2009.

to the Glory of God and for the edification of the body of Christ.

Taiwo Ogunsami is another mighty man for the Lord, passionate in the proclamation of the gospel and in the place of prayers. For this cause, he was one of the prayer champions who meet every Friday interceding for the church and the land. He was also part of the Flying Squad. Full of zeal for the Lord, he was sent to survey the city of Glasgow.

On the day, he walked around the city praying in the Holy Ghost all day and retired for the night at the bus stop. All these things were done selflessly unto the Lord. On his return from Glasgow, just like Caleb and Joshua, he was able to report: 'we are able to take Glasgow' for the Lord. With so much faith and zeal, he was sent forth with Segun Akinkugbe to Glasgow to start a church for the Lord. This was a task he worked on faith-

Ayo Akintomide is yet another man used mightily for the proclamation of the gospel. Although he is characteristically gentle and calm, he showed a great deal of determination for and dedication to the work of God. Given the coordinating role, he reorganised the House Fellowship, increased awareness among the brethren and encouraged members to be part of it.

JESUS HOUSE CITY OF GOD
FAMILY ROLL CALL

Abai Tina
Abana Osita
Abang Victoria
Abidakun Bisi
Abikoye Folashade
Abimbola Idowu
Abiodun Adefurin
Abiodun Taiwo
Abiodun Nwaosa
Abiola Bolu
Abiri Vivian
Abolarin John
Abolo-Tedi Judith Odion
Abolo-Tedi Nicholas
Aborowa Oludara
Abraham Awonuga
Abu George
Abugwu Victor
Adabiaka Olumide
Adams Jolomi
Adams Jolomi
Adams Missan
Adams Missan
Adebajo Jumoke
Adebanjo Kafayat
Adebayo Adeleke
Adebayo Alesanmi
Adebayo Kenny
Adebayo Kenny
Adebayo O Rotimi
Adebayo Olayinka
Adebayo Oluyomi
Adebayo Omolade
Adebayo Rotimi
Adebisi Yetunde
Adebiyi Rapheal
Adebiyi Rapheal
Adebodoye Wura
Adebola
Adegbesan
Adebowale
Akinbunmi
Adebule
Aderonke
Adedapo Yewande

Adedeji Adedayo
Adedeji Adeyemi
Adedeji Olaitan
Adedeji Oyepeju
Adedeji Peju
Adedesi King
Adedji Oyepeju
Adedoja Buki
Adedoyin Wuraola
Adefihan Kola
Adefihan Kola
Adegbesan Ifeoluwa Michael
Adegbotolu Abisola
Adegbotolu Oladipo
Adegbotolu Oladotun Vincent
Adegboyega Omoade
Adegoke Oluwatoyin
Adegoke Tobore Toyin
Adejoke Akinwale
Adejugba Ibukun
Adejumo Taiwo
Adekale Ibukun Hamed
Adekemi Debayo
Adekoya Kayode
Adekoya Yewande Joseph
Adekunle Dada
Adekunle
Adekunle Fagbenro
Adekunle Femi
Adekunle Funlola
Adekunle Ibitoye
Adekunle Oluwadunmade
Adekunle Opeyemi
Adekwu Nkechi
Adelakun Adeola
Adele Cituru
Adeleke Tayo
Adeleke Tayo
Adelusi Paul
Ademokoya

Afolayan Debo
Afolayan Theresa Tinuola
Afrifa Rapheal
Agba Arinze
Agbabune Henry
Agbaza K. J Simeon
Agbaza Simeon
Agbebaku-Izobo Isuan Mary Funke
Agboola Adebayo
Agboola Olawale
Agenmonmen Ejemen
Aghogho Aruoture
Agianpe Ashong
Agim Takon
Aguma Ogechi
Agunbiade Demola
Agunbiade Margret
Agunbiade Ruth
Agunbiade Sola Michael
Agwu Maclayton Ibiere
Ahimie Aye
Aiernakho Mercy Jatto
Aina Adetola
Aina Kehinde
Aina Yomi
Aiwannose Alex
Aja Beatrice
Ajaegbu Eberechi
Ajaiyi Samson
Ajani Ada-aku
Ajayi Adeyinka
Ajayi Ayokanmi
Ajayi Nike
Ajayi Nike
Ajayi Tobi
Ajayiobe Olusola
Ajayiobe Tejumade
Ajenifuja Tomson
Ajibade Tejumade
Ajibo Rebecca
Ajibo Rebecca
Ajibose Adeola

Ajibose Olusegun
Ajibose Titilayo
Ajiboso Oluyemi
Ajifolawe Ayodele
Aka Henry
Aka Ruby
Akan Richard
Akanbi Arinola
Akande Anu
Akande Ibukun
Akande Jimi
Akande Semilore
Akande Tonue
Akang Seuerema
Akanni Babatunde
Akanwoke Ngozi
Akaraiwe Afam
Akaraiwe Ivana
Akaraiwe Wendy
Akarakiri Femi
Akarakiri Nneka
Akasemi Oguru
Akawo Zainab
Akeju Ola
Akere Solomon
Akhimien Anthony
Akimoladu Mummy
Akinbo Elizabeth
Akinbode Adesola
Akinfolarin Ayotunde
Akingbade Biliki
Akinkugbe Halima
Akinkugbe Ibilola
Akinkugbe Oluseyi
Akinkugbe Segun
Akinlalu Daniel
Akinlalu Kunle
Akinlalu Kunle
Akinlalu Kunle
Akinlalu Tofunmi
Akinlalu Tolami
Akinlalu Tolani
Akinlalu Tomisi
Akinlemibola Oladayo
Akinleye
Akinrelere
Akinleye Cordelia

Akinrele Gloria
Akinrelere Idowu
Akinsanmi Deji
Akinsanmi Funmi
Akinsanya Temitopeoluwa
Akinseloyin Tinuke
Akintomide Ayo
Akintomide Folashade
Akintomide Jesudara
Akintomide Moyo
Akintomide Tofunmi
Akintude Dunmola
Akintundse Dunmola
Akinwale Adejoke
Akinwale Olubunmi
Akinwale Olubunmi
Akinwale Temilola
Akinwale Tobiloba
Akinyanmi Funke
Akinyele Akin
Akinyele Kemi
Akinyemi Arinola
Akinyo Ola
Akioya Edosa
Akioya Tokunbo
Akobo Agbani
Akobo Obelema
Akor Collin
Akuamoa Clarence
Akuanyionwu Uchechi
Akuanyionwu Uchechi
Akwafuo Sampson
Alao John
Alawa Gloria
Alekwe Osamwunyi
Alex-Adedipe Ronke
Alexander Umana

Alexandra Linsey
Alien Marie
Alika Funmi
Alistair Keith
Aliyu Okunene
Aliyu Olunene
Alles Antonet
Alliu Okoiza
Alliu Veronica
Alliu Veronica
Allwell-Brown Omosefe
Aloesa Dornubari
Aloke Aarlington
Aloke Chinwike
Aloke Oluchi
Aluebhosele
Aluebhosele Angela
Aluebhosele Angela
Aluebhosele Angela
Aluebhosele Obehi
Aluebhosele Steven
Aluebhosele Tony
Aluebhosele Tony
Aluko Kehinde
Alunyo Victoria
Alunyo Victoria
Ama Maud
Ama Nyimah
Amabipi Abby Kalio
Amadi Buduka
Amadi Charles
Amadi Chisa
Amadi Marvis
Amadi Richard
Amadi Richard
Amakiri Agana
Amaowoh Otobong
Amarachi Ogboi
Ame Utiome
Amedu Ugbede
Ameh Oche
Amelie Francois
Ameyo Kenneth
Amiator Quintine

Amike Abudu
Amike Faith
Amobi Eric
Amodu Fola
Amosu Yomi
Amugo Jane
Amugo Victor
Amu-Nnadi Onyiye
Anaekwe Maryann
Ananaba Kemijika
Anao Kingsley
Anderson Joyce
Anderson Rodney
Andrew Ekpekurede
Andrew Stewart
Anene Chinyelu Ifeanyi
Angyu Sherifat
Aniaka Augusta
Aniedi Umoh
Aniekan .C. Inyang
Anika Oluchi
Animashawun Bola
Animashawun Kola
Anipole Olawale
Aniyeloye Bethel
Aniyeloye Beulah
Aniyeloye Watson
Anjorin Adesiji
Anosike Chiedozie
Anozie Omuoha
Anthony Ejiro Oweh
Anthony Onunkwo
Anummu Chidimma
Anuopogena .O. Lucky
Anyeoziri Chijioke
Anyiam Sandra
Anzaku Esson
Ariba Olatayo
Arit Hilary John
Aro Oluwafemi
Aro Oluwfemi

Arogbofa Wande
Arojojoye Daniel
Arojojoye Kemi
Arojojoye Oluwakemi
Aruoture Aghogho
Aruwakoghe Orowo James
Asafa Sylvester
Asienga Irene
Asueifien Imo-Jack
Asuelimen Esele
Atabor Henry
Atabor Nkechi
Atamako Fegor
Atamako, Fegor.E
Atcaikni Erima
Attah Darah Albert
Attah Vincent
Augusta Awiaka
Avu Alfred
Awafung Stevens
Awafung Stewens
Awak Ufitofon
Awani Monisola
Awiaka Oluchi Laura
Awofiranye Taye
Awofisan Shadrack
Awomolo Oluwafemi
Awonuga Abraham
Awonuga Chide
Awonuga Tobi
Awopeju Toyin
Awopetu Abiola
Awote Sade
Awotorebo
Awoyade Tola
Awoye Lawson-Jack
Awoyemi Micheal
Ayakwo Ikechukwu
Ayanwu Stanley
Aye Ahimie
Ayede Sever
Ayerie Josephine
Ayettey Aisha
Ayilara Adetoun
Ayilaran Idowu Adeola
Ayoade Adegbite
Ayodeji Collins Lawal
Ayodeji Ogunlana
Ayodeji Olajide
Ayotunde Ogidom

Ayotunde Ogunkoya A
Azubike Obi
Azubike Lilian
Babalola Francisco
Babatope Kehinde
Babatope-Omoju Adeyemi
Babatunde Akanni
Babatunde Bolanle
Babatunde Lashore
Babatunde Olorunsogo
Babayiate Sangosanya
Babtunde Onilari
Bakare Tunde
Balogun Abib
Balogun Aminata
Balogun Angel
Balogun Lola
Balogun Omowunmi
Balogun Ove
Balogun Yinka
Bamgboye Layi
Bamidele Abiodun
Bamidele Seun
Bamidele Zizi
Bangura Kadiatu
Banjo Lola
Barajatya Dev
Barritor Gloria Alawa
Bawa Salka Daniel
Bazuaye Naomi
Bebey Jangwa
Bede Nwete
Bello Victor
Bello-Giwa Habiba
Bennett Patience
Bennette Patience
Bernard Eromosele
Bester Kabowanjete
Biola Adaramola
Bisola Jinadu
Blaseksen Victoria
Blessing Nwogu
Blogg Joe
Boadu A Kingsley
Boadu Amoakwa
Boma Lawson-Jack
Borg Anne-Gaelle
Boyle Prashad
Braide Michael
Brian Pay
Brian Rose
Bright Olusegun
Brizan Ketura

Buari Oluwabunmi
Buchi Atako
Bukola Oloko
Busola Abiola
Busola Sogbesan
Butkus Augustinas
Cachala Massoni
Callistus Muoneke
Camille Blin
Campbell Sarah
Cesarine Charles
Cesarine Divine
Chakraborty Anindya
Charles Ebienang
Chiboka Agape
Chide Awonuga
Chidebelu Chinenye
Chikani Isidore
Chima Chibueze
Chima Nzerem
Chimah Charity
Chimah Nduaguba
Chime Ezinne
Chinazom Chuks
Chinedu John
Chinemelim Kelvin
Chinwuko Victor
Chiweiri Mildred
Chiweyemba Ifeaka
Christina Dickson
Christine Osuigwe
Cindy Phillip
Cole Oluwatosin
Cole Oluwatosin
Cole Seun
Collins I Akor
Comfort Ndom
Cookery Muriel
Courage Onunkwo
D'Martins Chisa
Dada Adekunle
Dada Adekunle
Dadirai Agnes
Dagogo Omubo
Dagyeng Henry
Dallas Chichi
Damilanre Fapohunda
Damilola Odonfa
Danjubo Ifeoma
Danjuma Jude
Danjumbo Stefan
Dannow Steve
Dateme Ibiere
Datie-Ikoko Ebiikio
Daudu Emmanuel

Debakassa Jules
Debakassa Mary
Deekae Magdaiene
Deekae Peju
Deida Omoyeu
Delome Catherine
Dembo Musa
Dewotor Kafui
Dianne Stanley
Dibiaezue Uchechi
Dickson Stephanie
Dickson Vivian
Diete-Spiff Atonte
Digifa Bina
Digwo Pearl
Dimkpa Stanley
Dipe Emmanuel
Dire - Odukale Ayodeji
Dirisu David
Dominic Annie
Donna Louise
Dorunba Aloga
Douglas James
Douglas Tamunosaki
Douglas William
Douye Odi-Oweh
Dovydas Momkos
Duncan Eddie
Dzingina Susan
Dzvuke Tendai
Ebede Sylvester O
Ebienang Charles
Ebienang Charles
Ebienang Ekong
Ebienang Mary
Ebienang Mary
Ebimoghan Esther
Ebuta Oluchi
Echegiri Blessing
Edebiri Alaba
Edeniri Richard
Edewor Blessing
Edewor Orowo
Edi Braelatei
Ediagbonya Osahon
Edidiong Umoh
Edirisinghe Marian
Edosiem
Edward Obi
Edwin Isaiah
Efenovwe Emmanuel
Efeurhobo Austin
Egbejule Blessing
Egberongbe Ariyike

Egberongbe Ariyike
Egbo Chukwuemeka
Egbo Samuel
Egbo Samuel Chukwuemeka
Egekwu Ikoku
Egele Emenike
Egweh Elo
Ehidiamen Micheal
Ehikhale Gloria
Ejebu Clement
Ejiagwa Amaka
Ejike Ezejiofor
Ejikemeuwa Eric
Ejikemeuwa Nnanna
Ejim Chukwuka
Ejiro Oweh
Eka Anuonye
Ekahator Petra
Ekakitie Aderinola
Ekanem Enobong
Ekanem Etuk
Eke Helen
Eke Uchenna
Ekehon Alex
Ekehon Sandra
Ekere Othuke
Ekezie Chidinma
Ekom Ekom
Ekom Uyanga
Ekonye Nelson
Ekpemu Ugo
Ekpemu Uzo
Ekpiwhre Ejiro
Ekundayo Aruafu William
Ekundayo Musa
Ekweme Udoka
Ekwempu Ada
Eloagu Adora
Eloagu Chinedum
Eloagu Ngozi
Eloagu Vincent
Eloka Okoli
Elo-Oghene Egweh
Elufowoju Owojori
Eluwa Nnaemeka
Eluwa Nnemeka
Emegwa Tochukwu
Emejeamara Francis
Emeka Oduna
Emem James
Emem James

Emiehwe Ogaga
Emilolorun Olutosin
Emilorolun Bukola
Emilorolun David
Emilorolun Tosin
Emma Ibezim Kelechi
Emmanuel Abraham
Emmanuel Adejumo Oloyede
Emmanuel Oluseun Duro
Emmanuel Omotayo
Emuakpoterin Oyibo Walter
Enahoro Emmanuel
Enenche Felicia
Eniola Onafowokan
Enitinwa Kola
Enuma Daniel
Enwan Tony
Eremionkhale Isaac
Ernest Osemwinyen
Ero Iribhogbe
Eromosele Bernard
Eru Valmon
Esekhaigbe Idahosa Kelvin
Esekheigbe Idahosa
Eseoghene Etejere
Esezobor Eruvie
Esezobor Eruvie Evelyn
Esezobor Oluseyi
Esi Ribeiro
Esin Roland Kingsley
Esosa Bright Odigie
Essien Ikike
Essien Jessica
Essien Joyce
Essienumo Wkara
Etido Philip
Etim Akan R.
Etim Jonah
Etim Richard
Etta Josephine
Etuk Ekanem
Etulan Abang
Eunice Adesina
Evans Ron

Evwierhurhoma Roland
Ewanf Ekereobong
Eyeowa Jumoke
Eze Nwosu
Eze Onyekachukwu
Eze Robert Dilim
Ezechukwu Chinedu
Ezechukwu Chinenyeri
Ezechukwu Chinyeri
Ezeh Nwamaka Angela
Ezejiofor Chiemeka
Ezejiofor Ejike
Ezenwa Amara
Ezenwa Angela
Ezenwa Sasha
Ezeofor Chukwuemeka
Ezeogwa Alex Chinenye
Ezeola Chinemerem
Ezidiegimi Gerald
Ezioma Amechi
Ezra Panle
Ezubike Vivian
Ezurike Vivian
Fabiyi Moses
Fabunmi Ibukunoluwa
Fabusuyi Adedamola
Fadehan Lara
Fadehan Lara
Fadehan Omulara
Fadeyi Abidemi
Fadeyi Tina
Fagbemi Kehinde
Fagbenro Adekunle
Fagbenro Ramat
Fagbohun Temitope
Faith Suleiman
Fajonyomi Tope
Fakorede Titilayomi
Falade Oluwafunmilayo
Falana Gbemisola
Falconer Gloria
Falomo Adesola
Famoriyo Sola
Fanda Zigwai

Fapohunda Damilanre
Fasanmi Ajibola
Fasesin Omoniyi
Fashola olufunmilayo
Fasina Omotomilola
Fatugbo Babajide
Fatugbo Babajide
Faturoti Bukola
Faturoti Dolapo
Fayanjuola Ibukun
Fayomi Demola
Felisco Angelica
Femi Olorunshola
Fernandez Adesoji
Ferrecia Roselia
Ferrecia Roselia
Feuievia Joselia
Fiddo Fiddoson
Fidel Olu-Daudu
Filikunjombe Phillip
Fluorence Nkechi
Folami Olajumoke
Folasade Osisanya
Folashade Akintomide
Folorunso Adetayo Timothy
Fonweban Dennise
Fonweban John
Fonweban Rose
Francisco Babalola
Francisco Taiwo
Friday Aniefiok
Frodo-Edusei Zena
Funmi Isaac Sodeye
Funmilayo Fashola
Furo Ayebatonye
Furo Ruth
Furo Suoye
Gadima Chindaba
Gana Blessing
Gane Julius
Gbabo Esther
Gbahi Zoe
Gbarabe Leesi
Gbenga Gansallo
Gbolahan Taiwo
Gebremariam Isaiah
George Boyo
George Funmi
George Paul
George Taiwo
George Williamson

Gimu Hillary Betty
Gisele Ntumba
Ngela
Giwa Osage
Aigbangbe
Giwa-Osage Sidat
Giwa-Osage Sura
Giwa-Osagie Saliu
Gladys
Oluwadayomi
Gloria Ehikhale
Gloria Ileigo
Emmanuel
Gloria Soyele
Gocah Adriana
Godswill Isaiah
Goh Audrey
Goin Gaza
Grace Kemi
Oyewusi
Grace Kumah
Grahan Paul
Gurevin Alp
Gwuni E Evelyn
Habiba Yakubu
Hadiza Jibrin
Hasina Jansens
Helia Welwiteha
Hentle Jade
Hertlihy Elizabeth
Hew Alice
Hilary-John Arit
Hines Alesia
Hingston Stephen
Hong Gabriel
Ibano Doreen
Ibe Nnema
Ibeh Mayen
Ibifaa Iyalla
Ibikunle Oladipo
Ibikunle Tunde
Ibilola Ibikunle
Ibinabo Horsfall
Ibinabo Ngoye
Sunday
Ibrahim Aishatu
Auta
Ibrahim Kayode
Ibrahim Olufunke
Ibrahim Zainab
Auta
Ibudao Tobi

Ibukun Adejugba
Ibukun Adetona
Ibukunoluwa
Fabunmi
Idahosa
Esekhaigbe
Idehen Omoregie
Idiat Ogunbadejo
Idowu Bimbola
Idowu Damilola
Idowu Lekan
Idowu Oyinola
Idowu-Lade Bukky
Idowu-Lade Moses
Idundu Tuokpa
Ifaka Chiweyemba
Ifeanyi Ifeanyi
Ifenze Obinna
Ifeoma Francis
Nwogu
Ifezulike Chizzy
Ifezulike Jewel
Ifezulike Sonnie
Igbani Ikoro
Igbelokotor
Charles
Igbelokotor Ese
Igbelokotor Osa
Igbinosa Faith
Igbinovia
Norenegbe
Igho Ofodile
Igiehon Alero
Igiehon Mark
Igiehon Oghosa
Igiehon Osamagbe
Igiehon Uyiosa
Iginovia
Norenegbe
Igodo Kelvin
Igwe Adibe
Igweagbu Michael
Igwegbe Uzo
Igwegike Nebike
Iheanyi Blessing
Ihechukwu
Nwakibe
Ihim Emmanuel
Ihimoyan Rotimi
Ihinonsen A Steven
Ikeagu Chigozie
Ikeagu Ugochi
Ikediugwu
Chibuor
Ikena Ulasi
Ikepehai Tegah
Ikogho Eseoghene
Ikpehai Tegah
Ikukaiwe Ikechuku
Ikukaiwe

Ikechukwu
Ikukaiwe Nneka
Ikukaiwe Nneka
Ikukaiwe Nneka
Ikukaiwe Nneoma
Ikwuagwu
Chinedu Martins
Ikwunze Victoria
Ikyaagba Amos
Ikyaagbu
Iyoalumun
Ilechukwu Izundu
Ilechukwu Izundu
Ilechukwu Sidney
Ilias Lalos
Ilika Ugochukwu
Iloka Chidi
Iloka Chidi
Iloka Okpurhe
Vraye
Iloka Uche
Iloka Vraye
Ilori Seun
Ima Ibokette
Imediegwu
Charles
Imo – Jack
Asueifien
Imo Chinenye
Imo Juliet
Imoh Ifiok
Imonieroh
Ejiroghene
Imonige Josephine
Imonige Larry
Imonigie Josephine
Imonigie Lawrence
Imonigie Lawrence
Imonikhe Thomas
Iniobong Usen
Inok Joseph
Inyang Clement
Inyang Michael
Inyang Ubong
Irbhogbe Ama
Maud
Iroegbu Nathaniel
Irotumhe Aleobe
Joseph
Isaac-Sodeye F
Isaiah Goodswill
Isaiah Rachel
Isaiah Rachel
Ishabiyi Francis
Ishola Ibukunolu
Isiah Obe
Isioma Okpoli
Isong Utoro
Iteye Ogbo
Itim Vivian

Iwayemi Oshe
Iwe Ikenna
Azubike
Iwelomen Patience
Iwelomen Patience
Iwenofu Chuchu
Iweze Isabella
Iwobi Fred Obiora
Iyalla Boma
Iyaagbu
Iyalla David
Iyalla Ibifaa
Iyalla Ibiye
Iyamu Osayi Peter
Iyelabola Kimberly
Iyinbor Victor
Izebizua Paul
Izima Obinna
Izu Nnabuife
Izzi Elomobo
J. E Asuguo
Jackson-Cole J
Jadesola Francis
Jagboro A. Bryne
Jagboro Bryne
Jagobinora Rita
Jaja Isreal
Jaji Tolulope
Jatto Airenakho
Jegede Bolaji
Jimoh Abisoye
Jimoh Oluyinka
Jimoh Oluyinka
Jimoh Shope
Jinadu Olanrewaju
Jinadu Oyepero
Jitte Chinomao N
Jobome Joy
John Mark
Johnson
Oluwasegun
Johnson-Williams
Bonnie
Joke Aderemi
Joseph Itodo
Emmanuel
Julius Ayo
Kabowanjete Bester
Kafula Nelly
Kalu Emmanuel
Kalu O Emmanuel
Kamukalan
Richard
Kanu Godfrey
Karikari Koi Afum
Kasemo Temitope
Kato Veronica
Kayode Sadiq
Kechukwu Sidney
Kedziora
Magdalena

Keith Alastair
Kelechi Emma-
Ibezim
Kelechi Uche
Kemmonye Ngaka
Kerry Rachel
Kesime Janet
Kevin Abu
Kevwe Kofi
King Ryan
Kingsley Enem
Kio Fredrick
Kirk Betsy
Kirk Ella
Kirk Magret
Kofoworola
Shoyinka
Kola
Animashawun
Kola Enitinwa
Kolade Oluwatosin
Kola-Olalere Esther
Kikelomo
Kole-Emmanuel
David
Komolafe Segun
Konlan Vinenyoh
Kperegbeyi Esther
Kperegbeyi Yemi
Krakwa Richard
Kristine McDonald
Krukrubo Opiribo
Krukrubo-Karibi
Morgan
Kuku Abimbola
Kulor Frank
Kumah Mimi
Grace
Kunadu Conrad
Kyabagwu
Ramona
Labeodan Femi
Ladeinde Dami
Ladejobi Sade
Laidler Tracy
Larry Ekpudu
Lashore Babatunde
Laural Annie
Lawal Adetola
Lawal Akeem
Lawal Ayo
Lawal Dami
Lawal Dapo
Lawal Folunke
Lawal Ronke
Lawal Tayo
Lawal Temi
Lawal Tito
Lawal Tolu
Lee Judy

Leich Graeme
Leitch kate
Lesole Ngaka
Lirubusi Jerry
Lobo Lorena
Loluja Agbani
Akobo
Longe Abraham
Louis Fabiola
Louis Isaac
Loveline Obi
Lumati
Ugochukwu
Lutumba Ingrid
Iymmy Ogbidi
MacDonald
Kenneth
MacDonald Steven
MacDonald Steven
J
MacInned Roddy
Maclayton Erefaa
MacLennan Jessica
MacRac Lynette
Madu David
Madu Irene
Madu Johannes
Madu John
Madu Onii
Magaji Adams
Mahuya Simba
Mair Diana
Maliya Ngalam
Manguez Bridget
Mania Vasco
Mante Priscilla
Manyatsa Dikano
Maples Victor
Maples Victor
Masoni Smart
Matthew
Emuemhonjie
Matthew Sarah
Mbadihe Chinonso
Mbaso Amaka
Mbeh Abel
Mbeh Maimuna
Mclaughlin
Michael
Mclaughlin Regina
McMillian Alana
McNish Christina
Mekwuye
Onyemaechi
Meme Victor
Menugba Onyeka
Meze Hyacinth
Mfune Oleans
Mina Manuel
Mobolaii Avoade

Mogba Bosede
Mogba John
Molake Abiola
Momkute Ioana
Momoh Majester
Monica Opiyo
Montez Wandick
Monyei Ikenna
Monyei Monyei
Morenike onayemi
Moses Okan
Moses Sokunbi
Mowo Obe
Moyo Pauline
Mrs Ayebatonye
Muasya Paul
Mudramin Nolish
Mugo Elizabeth
Mukherjee
Seemanti
Mumie
Shangpliang
Musa Dembo
Musa Ekundayo
Musa Vera
Mutombo Kalala
Franc
Mutyora-Gwati
Loreta
Mutyora-Gwati
Loreta
Muyiwa
Olayiwola
Muyiwa Akinbode
Nadlambudzi
Pamda Queen
Najar Dennis
Nakawala Mirriam
Nakayenga
Cynthia
Nakimbugwe
Charlotte
Nakimbugwe
Charlotte
Nbanusi
Onyebuchi
Ndagire Laureene
Ndebueze Linda
Ndubude
Obidigwe
Nduka Raps
Nege Joseph
Ngela Chris
Ngela Chris
Nimiten Henry
Nimyel Jennifer
Niteh Kingsley
Niyi Adebayo
Njoku Joanne
Njoku

Kenechukwu
Njoku Mitchelle
Njoku Obinna
Njoku Uzoma
Njokubi Ndidi
Nkebakwe
Basimefune
Nkebakwe Patricia
Nkebakwu Kelechi
Nkebakwu Kevin
Nkechi Obika
Nliam Ngozi
Nnabuife
Izuchukwu
Nnaji Amarachi G
Nnoji Emila
Noma Garrick
Nonye Agbaza
Ntepu Julliet
Ntuk Idongesit
Ntumba Gisele
Nukaka Alice
Nurudeen Oladapo
Nurudeen
Oluwatoyin
Olurike
Nwachukwu Elvis
Nwachukwu
Oluchi
Nwaebee Dominic
Nwafor
Chukwuemeka
Nwafor Ndubisi
Nwagor Paulinus
Waiwu Gallabeth
Nwaiwu Ugochi
Nwakanma Bon
Ugo
Nwakubo Chioma
Nwalozie Alozie
Nwando Aghamya
Nwankwo Obinna
Nwanna Chioma
Nwanna Ral
Nwanne Ikenna
Nwanne O Cynthia
Nwanze Jenifer
Nwanze Nancy
Nwaor
Chukwuemeka
Nweke Jason
Nweke
Toberchukwu
Nwerenga Alice
Nwete Vivian
Nwete Vivian
Nwinee Lawrence
Nwinee Sara
Nwobodo Ojay
Nwogu Blessing

Nwogu Chukuemeka
Nwogu Ibiye
Nwoknota Chiadi
Nwosah Miriam
Nwosu Oluchi
Nwouya Mac-donald
Nwuwa Ugochukwu
Nyambura Mercy
Nyateka Tafiee
Nyimah Ama
Nzekwe Talatu
Nzelu Ikechukwu
Nzelu Ikechukwu
Nzerem Chimah
Nzewi Amaka
Nzewunwa Ikenna
O'Samuel Anwli
O'Samuel Jed
Obakpolor Simon Nosa
Obamo Bukky
Obariase Efosa
Obaro Efe
Obaro Isoken Anita
Obaro-Okpopkor Uzezi
Obasi Oluseyi
Obasi Oluseyi
Obasuyi Eghosasere
Obasuyi Tracy
Obe Otakore
Obehi Aluebhosele
Obelema Akobo
Obi Edward
Obi Ikechukwu
Obi Ikechukwu
Obi Joy
Obi Loveline
Obi Samuel
Obiade Josephine
Obiagwu Sunny-Joe
Obidimalor I Nelson
Obidimalor Iyke
Obidimalor Emmanuel Precious
Obiefuna Jideobi
Obikili Ejidike
Obodoekea Patrick
Oboh Joseph
Obomate Obomate
Obonna Omonigho
Obonna Uyavie
Obude Olufemi

Ochekpe Daniel
Ochie Chude Winston
Ochie Joe
Ochonba N Sidney
Ode Jennifer
Odega Ebuni
Odeh Tessa
Oderinde Kayode
Odesanya Oluwalemi
Odetoyinbo Kayode
Odiakose E Adigwe
Odibo Onome
Odigie Collins
Odigie Esosa
Odikagbo Uche
Odikagbo Uche
Odikose Eziafakego
Odina Chibuzor
Odion Ikhide
Odion Ikhide
Odi-Owei Douye
Odum Joseph
Odumodu Uzoma Chigozie
Odumosu Calton
Oduna Emeka
Odunaya Otele
Odunfa Damilola O
Oduse Kayode
Odusola Kayode
Ofem Mary
Offiong Offiong
Offiong Orok
Ofgba Pamela
Ofodile Igho
Ofodili Chikadibia
Ofogba Sylvester
Ogaji Florence
Ogamba Ugochukwu
Ogbalu Ebele
Ogbeifun Louis
Ogbeifun Nime
Ogbidi Ighodalo Emmanuel
Ogbo Iteye
Ogbobe Buko
Ogbodo Onuorah
Ogbodo Uju
Ogbomo Precious
Ogbonda Chidi
Ogbonna Kingsley
Ogbonnaya Achara
Ogboruche Chinedum

Ogboruche Chinedum
Ogboruche Favour
Ogbouche Caleb
Ogbu Chibuzor
Ogbuekwe Mike
Ogbulu Kingsley
Ogedengbe Abimbola
Ogedengbe Dunsimi
Ogedengbe Iyiola
Ogedengbe Philip
Ogedengbe Timothy
Oghenekevwe Kofi
Oghenekevwe Ogaga
Ogidan Ayotunde
Ogina Olivier
Ogina Sarah
Ogu Daniel
Ogundadejo Idiat
Ogundewo Yewande
Ogundimimi Bukola
Ogundipe Kunle
Ogunduyile Modupe
Ogunfidodo Aderinola
Ogunfidodo Mabel
Ogunkola Anu
Ogunkoya Oluwatosin
Ogunkunle Omololu Frank
Ogunlana Ayodeji
Ogunleye Adebukonla
Ogunleye Adeyomi
Ogunmola Beatrice
Ogunmola Beatrice
Ogunmola Michael
Ogunmola Victor
Ogunmola Victor
Ogunmosu Elizabth
Ogunsakin Remi
Ogunsanya Adejimi
Ogunsanya Kunle
Ogunsola Yomi
Oguntade taiwo
Oguntodu Princess
Oguntodu Seun
Oguntodu Seun

Oguntola Bunmi
Oguntoye Ademola
Ogunyemi Ayodeji Amos
Ogunyemi Rotimi
Oguru Akasemi
Ohunene Aliyu
Oje Bello
Oje Michael
Ojeaburu Edeifo
Ojemakinde Bukola
Ojiako Harachi
Ojiako Jachi
Ojiako Kamsi
Ojieh Chuks
Ojijiagwo Chichi
Oji Stephen
Ojo Esther
Ojo Kemi
Ojo Michael
Ojo Omotayo
Ojo Omotayo
Ojo Opeyemi Itunu
Ojo Oyinlola
Ojoboh Onome
Ojuile Tobiloba
Oukonsin Tebe
Ojukwu Chinwe
Ojukwu Paul
Okafor Golibe
Okafor Charles
Okafor Emeka
Okafor Happiness
Okafor Juanita
Okafor Odinaka
Okafor Roselin
Okafor Valentine
Okafor Valentine
Okan Moses
Okaroh Ifeoma
Oke Okah-Avae
Oke Seye
Oke Seye
Oke Toye
Okechukwu Divinegift
Okechukwu Emeka
Okechukwu Nnaemeka
Okechukwu Obiageli Mary
Okeke Afamefuna
Okeke Judith Chika
Okemuote Oyo
Okeoghene

Ugbehe
Okeoma Daniel
Okereke Emmanuel
Okereke Emmanuel
Okerinde Bola
Okerinde Bunmi
Okerinde David
Okerinde Jide
Okerinde Olaide
Okerinde Temitope
Okerinde Titi
Okewumi Mayowa
Okewunmi Ayodeji
Okey Ijeomah
Okhiria Christopher
Oklobia Ochai
Oko Bonahis
Okoli Chinenye
Okoli Josephine
Okolie Uzor Sunday
Okon Oto
Okonicha Roland
Okonicha Ugo Roland
Okonji Samuel
Okonjolu Toyin
Okonkwo Emmanuel
Okonkwo Vincent S

Okorji Uchechukwu
Okoroafor Chidinma
Okoroafor Ijeoma
Okoroafor Praise
Okoroafor Ugonna
Okoroafor Vanessa
Okoroji Darlington
Okoronkwo Augusta
Okosun Vivian
Okougha Dami
Okougha Darlington
Okougha Ehime
Okougha Modupe
Okoungha Ose
Okpagu Nonso
Okpako Andrew
Okpako Andrew-Ena
Okpebholo Onomen

Okpo Emmanuel
Okpopkor Obaro
Okulaga Ololade
Okulaji Ololade
Okundiya Dolapo
Okuneye Oluwajuwan
Okuneye Oluwajuwonlo
Okuneye Olumuyiwa
Okuneye Oluwayuwinlo
Okunjolu Toyin
Okunkwo Joseph
Okunuga Jeshron
Okunuga Precious
Okunuga Sola
Okurinboye Olajide
Okuyelu Gbemisola
Olabode Kehinde
Olabode Margret
Olabuile Austin
Oladeji Lola
Oladimeji Bashorun
Oladimeji Samuel
Oladipo Abimbola
Oladipo Adegbotolu
Oladipo o. Gbenle
Oladokun Afolake
Oladugba Odunayo

Oladunmi Odanye
Olaegeb Tolulope
Olagunju Abiodu
Olagunju Adeyemi
Olagunju Jefe
Olaia Charles
Olaitan .T. Adedeji
Olajide Okerinde
Olajumoke Folami
Olakitan Olowoyo
Olakunle Boma
Olakunle Onyinye
Olaleye Lanre
Olanrewaju A-Cole
Olanrewanju Dami
Olanrewanju Dapo
Olanrewanju Timi
Olanrewanju Toyin
Olaogun Lanre
Olaoya Taiwo
Olatinsu Gbemisola
Olatinsu Olamide
Olatinsu Oluwabusola

Olatunji Tayo
Olawale Nurrudeen
Olawale Omoniyi
Olawoyin Olaniyi
Olawuni Michael
Olayiwola Kemi
Olayiwola Kemi
Olayiwola Olumuyiwa
Olekah Bruce
Olife Gabriel
Oliyide Olufumilayo
Ologunleko Modupe
Ololade Okulaja
Olomola Gbenga
Olorode Olekan
Olowe Olugbenga
Olowodaran Dapo
Olowojoba Gani
Olowole Gbenga
Olowoyo Adebusola
Olubiyi Toyin
Olubodun Bola
Olubola Olusanya
Oludinmu Oluwadami
Oludipe Tobi
Olufemi Fasoro
Olufemi Morenike
Olufunke David
Olufunmilayo Fashola
Olugboji Moyo
Olujide Tomi
Olujimi Temitope
Olujinmi Akinkunmi
Olukanmi Tosin
Olukunle Ezekiel
Olunsegun Abimbola
Olunyo Adelayi
Olusegun Kolawole
Olusegun Toyin
Oluseyi Michael
Olushola Kehinde
Olusimi Akande
Olusola Ledun
Oluwadayomi Jide
Oluwaseun Kayode
Oluwaseyi Olayinka
Oluwatayo Stephen
Oluwabusola

Oluwateru Damilola
Oluwateru Oladotun
Oluwateru Yetunde
Oluwatosin Ogunkoya
Oluwole Olaseni O
Oluwole Omokayode
Omabiyi Abiodun
Omagbemi Toyin
Omejalile Terry Matthew
Omeje Uchenna
Omikunle Tokunbo
Omiragwa Jite
Omiraywadia Gladys
Omiyale Jerry
Omo Ashion
Omobude Faith
Omoediale Anwuli
Omofade Adegboyega
Omofoye F A
Omogbami Toju
Omoge Lola
Omoge Omolola
Omogun Omoniyi
Omohowho O Okoro
Omoju Bolaji
Omoju Olajinka
Omokwale Hope
Omolayo Osasona
Omole Deola
Omole Ebuoluwa
Omole Folasade
Omole Helen
Omole Wunmi
Omomowo Olumide
Omonigho Obniwerbe
Omoniyi Eseosa
Omonkalo Meshack
Omoregie Clement
Omoregie Idehen
Omoregie Isoken
Omoregie Isoken
Omoregie Precious
Omoregie Rogie
Omoruyi Josephine
Omosalewa Akin
Omosebi

Oyindamola
Omotomilola
Torera
Omuederiaye
Emmanuel
Omuederiaye
Emmanuel
Omuregie Rogie
Ona Ikuba John
Onafeko Fisola
Onafeko Folajimi
Onafeko Samson
Onafowokan
Eniola
Onafowokan
Temitayo
Onajin Tolulope
Onakanmi John
Onakanmi Nike
Onamade Sean
Onamade Tunde
Onamade Yvonne
Onamuti
Monturayo
Onatuga Olufemi
Onayemi Morenike
Oni Gbemisola
Oni Morenikeji
Oni Wale
Onikoyi Dotun
Onilari Babatunde
Onkonkwo Uche
Onochie Nkechi
Onoja Marcus
Onunkwo Anthony
Onuoha Michael
Onwukamike
Marvelous
Onwuzurike Zeph
Onyeabo G
Onyebuchi
Mafiana
Onyebuchi
Okereke
Onyeche Nosegbe
Onyeka Nneka
Onyeka Nneka
Onyekwere Ijeoma
Onyekwere
Chibuzor
Onyekwere Gloria
Onyekwere Jones C
Onyemaechi
Mekwuye
Onyewueke Ela
Onyewueke Judah
Onyewueke
Osemwinyen
Ernest
Unique
Onyewueke Zoe
Onyiwe Bernard

Onyiye Amu-
Nnadi
Opara Chinyere
Opara-Martins
Chris
Oparandu Chinwe
Oparene Samuel
Ope Lawrence
Ope Lawrence
Orafidiya Folake
Orakwue Amaka
Orakwue Amaka
Orenuga Paul
Oriaifo Odianosen
Orike Sunny
Orire Sumibola
Oritsemeyin
Osibeluwo
Oriunuebho
Andrew
Oriunuebho
Chidinma
Oriunuebho
Goodness
Oriunuebho Great
Orivri Sophia
Orji Fidelia
Arunma
Orji Ikechukwu
Orji Temple
Chukwuemeka
Orogo Adewale
Orok Offiong
Orubusi Kenneth
Orubusi Kenneth
Oruche Amaka
Oruche Amaka
Osadola Tolulope
Osaghae Divine
Osaghae Faith
Osaghae Joseph
Osagie
Ikponmwosa
Osagie Isi
Osahon Sike
Osakwe Adora
Osakwe Aluka
Osakwe Howard
Osanyin
Olatundun
Osarieme Thelma
Omoruyi
Osasona Omolayo
Osasona Tayo
Osasona Temitope
Osasona Tope
Osezua Kenneth
Osezua Ogudo

Oyejonpo Oyenuga
Oyeniyan Bukola
Oyenuga Jonpo
Oyeronke Ladapo
Oyeronke Theresse
Oyewole Lola
Oyewusi
Oluwakemi
Oyindamola
Oyinlola
Oyinebragha
Olobio
Oyom Maxwell
Ozoemena Amechi
Ozoemena Ifeoma
Ozugha
Chukwuebuka
Pang Matthew
Pearce Emma-Jane
Pearce Emma-Jane
Pedro Jadesola
Pepple Sarah
Peter Ehiabor
Petra Ekhator
Pevera Anthony
Pevera Francisca
Pevera Rohan
Philips Aderonke
Phillips Olufunto
Pollard Alan
Popoola
Oluwatimilehin
Precious Faith
Osuigwe
Preetha Alexander
Priscilla Olawuyi
Psazde John
Puddu Laura
Quintine-Amiator
Nkechi
Rachwalik Janusz
Rahuan Sujida
Ratnasatapthy
Sarah
Ratnasatapthy
Thevarjah
Reiner Van Der
Ryst
Rivkah Maya
Rogie Omeregie
Ross Brian
Ruhaak Ray
Rutherford Emma
Sagay Owunmi
Sagay Ufuoma
Saheed Adebola
Saletu Elisa
Sample Klarke
Sampson Akan Eno
Samuel Elizabeth

Samuel Stella
Samuel Yemi
Sandy Surtees
Sanni Bolaji
Sanni Deji
Sanni Makinde
Sanni Roger
Santos Egbon
Saula Bukky
Segun Ajibose
Sekerema Akang
Senlong Katmaan
Sethare Vicyor
Shamgpliang
Mumie
Shaun Carroll
Shittu Uchechi
Shobowale
Oluseun
Shode Abimbola
Shofola Tunde
Shola Janet
Siam Kocakqpbn
Sigbeku Timi
Simeon Agada
Siminialayi
Iwarimie
Siminialayi Steven
Simon Ewaoche
Sini Tumba
Sipeolu Oluwaseun
Francis
Sipeolu Seun
Smith Rosmary
Sogbesan Busola
Sokunbi Moses
Sonalo SJ
Sonuga Kunle
Sowemimo
Adewale
Soyebo Michael
Olusesan
Soyele George
Soyingbe
Adegboyega
Soyingbe Damilola
Soyingbe Joseph
Stanley Okonkwo
Steel Matthew
Stephen Kwelle
Sulle Anthony O
Surtees Cassie
Surtees Christy
Tade Oyewunmi
Tade Oyewunmi
Tade Tolu
Taiwo Adetola
Taiwo Titi
Takpi Seyi Lucky
Talabi Funke

Talabi Kehinde
Omolara
Tanga Joy
Tavershma Ayede
Taylor Elizabeth
Temitayo
Onafowokan
Temitope Akiode
Teslim Iyabo
Thompson Victor
Thorton David
Tochukwu Obika
Tokode Abiola
Folorunso
Tolbert Kelvin
Tolulope Jaji
Tolulope Olaegbe
Tombari Aadum
Tomilola kayoed
Torty Kalu-ulu
Toshar Phalak
Tosin Ojumu
Tunba Dini
Tunde Onamade
Tunde-Anjous
Abioye
Tuokpe Idundun
Turnbull Joan
Turnbull Robert
Ubia Ini Ubia
Ubong Enem
Ucari Fiona
Uche Anayo
Uche Kelechi
Uche Kelechi
Uche Nnenna
Uche Onyikwu
Uchechi Dibiaezue
Uchendu Chinwe
Uchenna
Nwankwo
Ude Nonso
Udeaja T Ifeanyi
Udeme Udosen
Udeze Stella
Udo Nkechinyere
Udo Udo
Udok Regina
Udok Kufre
Udosan Udeme
Uduebholo
Patience
Udusegbe Temi
Ufuk Bircan
Ugbo Daniel
Ugochukwu
Chijioke
Ugonna Okoroafor
Ugun Clifford
Uguru Obinna

Ugwoke Christian
Ugwu Clifford
Ugwu Clifford
Ugwulashi
Godstime
Ukaejiofo
Amarachi
Ukandu Chidi
Ukandu Jjeoma
Ukhun Patrick
Ukpong Daniel
Ulasi Stanley
Umana Alexander
Umeh Isreal
Umeh Isreal
Umeh Richard
Umeh Yinka
Umejei Chuks
Umerie Chinwe
Umoh Amiedi
Umoh Chinenye
Umoh Edidiong
Umoh Idara Akpan
Umoh Idongesit
Umoh Inemesit
Umoh Iniobong
Umoh Udeme
Umudjoro David
Umudjoro Ivana
Umudjoro Kenneth
Umudjoro Ruth
Unabor Tinuke
Grace
Urubusi Jerry
Urubusi Jerry
Urum Christine
Urum Princewill
Urumedji Faith
Usiagwu Efemena
Utchay-Okorji
Sogba
Uwadileke Vincent
Uwah Ifiok A
Uwah Ifiok A
Uwaifo Kes
Uwalaka Chinyere
Uwom Chinedu
Uwom Emeka
Uwom Umunna
Uwubanmwen Uyi
Uyanga Ekom
Uzah Christian
Uzoechina Obinma
Uzoechina Obinma
Uzokwe Franklin
Uzoma Lovela
Uzoukwu Obinna
Uzu Esther
V.C Abugwij
Vanderveldes Faith

West Pamela
West Pamela
William Bambo
William Banke
Williams Esther
Williams Kayode
Williams Rita
Williamson
Chineye
Williamson George
Wojuade
Adebuloka
Wolo Preiye
Wolo Tlmi
Wonuola Scott
Wonuola-Scott
Olaitan
Wopara Chioma
Worlu Ighechi
Wuraola Motayo
Xing Hu
Yakubu Abigail
Yakubu Divine
Yakubu Victor
Yakubu Victor
Yardua Lola
Yejide Onabule
Yemisi Oguntoye
Yetty Thomoson
Yewande Adedapo
Yewande Adekoya
Yinka Umeh
Yisau Muideen
Alade
Ynieto Bernadine
Yupah Joe
Yusuf Micah
Zabadi Kahassa
Zadi Gisele
Zainad Usman
Natasha
Ziafa Adegwe
Zikawe Nakatindi
Zikawe Pablo
Zikawe Ridley
Zubi - Emele
Adaeze
Zubi - Emele
Chimdi
Zubi – Emele
Onyedikachi

Igiehon Family
Meze Family
Caleb Ogboruche
Family
Odunlami Family
Akinmoladun
Family
G K Olotu Family

CHILDREN CHURCH

A scene of the children's drama

Another scene of the children
performing their drama

A scene of the children's drama

Children church performs a
drama for the adults

Children cutting their cake - 2008

Santa hands out christmas present to
Fara while Dunsimi wait

Children having fun of children's day 2008

MORE PENIEL PICTURES

JH MEMBERS VIEW CITY OF GOD AFTER BUILDING PURCHASE

Also, he started and championed the Flying Squad and through it, he started a church in Elgin. Through his zeal and testimony, he ministered to the community of Elgin and this led to the restoration of lives and winning of souls for the kingdom. His missionary work in Elgin city was very fruitful especially among the local community as the church had more than 50 percent locals in the congregation. He had a heart for the people, was very temperate in all things and dedicated in his work. He continued in his work for the Lord until he relocated to Canada in 2010. Today, the Flying Squad is coordinated by Tosin Emilolorun.

Another man who is selfless in his service to the community, the people and the church is **Obaro Okpokpor and his wife Uzezi.** He dedicated himself to the follow-up of brethren and new converts. Through his service a lot of members made Jesus House Aberdeen their home. His wife is also worthy of great commendation. She started the children church and continued as the pastor of the children church up till the day she relocated with her husband to Nigeria. Their service to God and the people was faultless. They were also involved in church planting at Inverness to the glory of God. They supported Jesus House Aberdeen in many ways including administration, yielding their lives totally to God and ensuring the welfare of the ministry. Like Obaro Okpokpor always said, "God does not owe any man" and indeed, God rewarded and continues to reward them greatly for their service in His kingdom.

Time and space will not allow us to name the mighty men and women who have done and continues to do great exploits. People like Pastor Selere, Solomon Akere and so on. The list on the next page shows those who are part of God's great army.

JESUS HOUSE ABERDEEN 7ᵀᴴ YEAR ANNIVERSARY

SECRETS FROM GOD'S CONSTRUCTION SITE

God wants us to impact lives

2 Samuel 22, gives the account of David and his mighty men. Originally, these were men discontented, in debt and distressed. But after their encounter with David and the God of David, their lives were changed forever.

> And every one that was in distress, and every one that was in debt, and every one that was discontented, gathered themselves unto him; and he became a captain over them: and there were with him about four hundred men.- 1Samuel 22. 2 (KJV)

In our service, God wants us to influence lives of the people that come our way. The light of God in our lives should transform and change the people we encounter. In Jesus House, God has helped Pastor Mark Igiehon and the team of Ministers to positively influence the lives of the people that visit and worship at Jesus House positively.

We can do exploits for our King

Just like David and his men, God want us to do great exploits for him. David's mighty men did more than David did in his own time. One of them killed Goliath's brother who was greater in size than Goliath. So we should do great exploits for God in our generation and time.

There are rewards for serving the King

Another secret we have learnt from our work with God is that God blesses us when we work for Him with all our heart. He is a rewarder of those who diligently seek him. When we work for God, he blesses us.

The testimonies of those who have been instrumental to the work of God in Jesus House Aberdeen, for example, show that God blessed and promoted them beyond their imagination and thoughts. This indicates that those who work for God have great rewards.

PENIEL 2009

Chapter 10

SHOWCASING THE KINGDOM

THE MAGAZINE MINISTRY

As Jesus House Aberdeen grew and increased in her fame abroad, a host of people were unaware of her goals, objectives and benefits to the community. In order to effectively communicate to the people, publications became a necessary medium to communicate to the community what the church represents; hence, the birth of the publication unit and the commencement of the magazine ministry. The magazines explain what God is doing in us, for us and through us. The inaugural edition was published in June 2007.

Front pages of the different editions of City of God Magazine

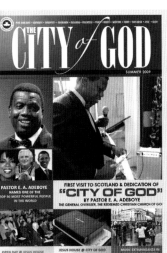

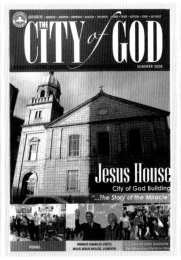

This is what the Editor-in-Chief had to say in his foreward in the inaugural edition:

WELCOME TO THE CITY
FOREWARD BY PASTOR MARK OSA IGIEHON

Welcome to *The City of God*, an exciting publication which is a testament to the eternal truth that 'with God, all things are possible. Thanks to God for the vision, divine enablement, resources and the wonderful team that brought this magazine to reality. The magazine you hold in your hands is the result of a vision that took well over two years to come to fruition. It took many fits and stops for this magazine to reach publication. If you have visions, plans and expectations that appear to be delayed, I encourage you, do not give in or give up; instead, keep at it, work at it, keep nursing it, look unto the Lord and be quick to recognize and utilize divinely arranged opportunities and resources to see your vision come to fruition. Though it lingers, wait for it!

Why the 'City of God'? Today we live in times when it appears that matters of the Kingdom are being pushed out of daily and society life. It appears that God Himself is now considered almost as an anachronism by some and with bitter personal contempt by a host of others. Many in our society live under the impression that the British society and civilization has 'outgrown' God and that ours is now a post-Christian society. It is unfortunate and very damaging that a society, nation and civilization that owes successes in its heritage, civilization, advancement and ethos to its Christian heritage now assumes that it has outgrown God and Christianity. Simon Heffer (a self proclaimed atheist) in the Daily Telegraph of Saturday 17th February 2007 lamented:

'I have a concern for the Church ... Our economic development was helped by this country's conversion to Protestantism, and the liturgy of the Church ... is one of our greatest cultural treasures'.

We know from history that when a nation or people forsake and forget their Lord and God, it is only a matter of time before great spiritual and moral emptiness sets in. As there is no vacuum in heaven or nature, the spiritual and moral emptiness gives way for high spates of ungodliness which in turn wrecks great havoc on the very fabric of nation, society, and family. Ancient Israel found it to be true that distancing from God always led to weakening of the State and breakdown of society.

A recent survey has identified the United Kingdom as the worst place in the western affluent world to raise children, due to breakdown of marriages and families, etc. Juxtaposing the UNICEF reports that with accounts of drunken youths and elders; so many addicted to drugs; young children in drug filled homes for whom it will take the grace of God for them to be of any use to themselves or the society, it becomes immediately clear that we in Britain, if we do not retrace our ways could 'sleep-walk' into our own version of Armageddon, our own version of Rome burning while Nero fiddles. I am reminded that our situation today is so fitly described in scriptures:

What happened was this: People knew God perfectly well, but when they didn't treat him like God, refusing to worship him, they trivialised themselves into silliness and confusion so that there was neither sense nor direction left in their lives. They pretended to know it all, but were illiterate regarding life ... So God said, in effect, "If that's what you want, that's what you get." It wasn't long before they were living in a pigpen, smeared with filth, filthy inside and out. (Romans 1.18-25, the Message)

It is interesting that the press, politicians and even government itself, assert that the problem is that of the government and therefore that the government can sort it all out. How very mistaken! The government and politicians have undoubtedly contributed towards the problem. Recall the recent debate on whether Church agencies should be compelled to act contrary to Biblical beliefs and standards. Those are the types of policies that together delivered the state of family, marriage and society that we live in today. Government and politicians do not have all the answers.

The Church, as an institution in recent times, has largely failed to serve as a backbone as well as provide clear spiritual and moral direction to the nation and society. That, to a large extent, is the root cause of the state of society today. If the Church once again assumes its proper role as it did in years and centuries past and government and society, begin once more to simply respect and fear God and work towards the promotion of those vital institutions of God (such as marriage), then, we will be on the right track back to the type of cohesive society that we really need. We need to return to the faith of our fathers.

So the *City of God* is designed to showcase the Lord and His church and its place in present society; to show its relevance to everyday life; a forum for the practical application of the word of God to successful everyday living. It is aimed at children, young and older and indeed every facet of society. You will find something in here for you. Read it, share it, talk about it and tell us about your experience and views. If you have any questions, please send them in and we will both respond as well as publish some of the questions and responses in future editions.

Enjoy it and may we together make our nation, societies and cities once more like the City of God.

EDITORIAL FOR 2008
CITY OF GOD MAGAZINE
BY PASTOR MARK OSA IGIEHON

WHAT A WONDERFUL GOD WE SERVE!

At the beginning of year 2007, we could not have imagined what great heights in individual lives and together as a church, the Lord intended to take us. At the end of the year and looking back at the year 2007, we are so overwhelmed by the glory and majesty of our Lord. To Him alone be the glory. We saw people getting saved, lives changed, deeper communion with the Lord, transformations, marriages turned around, diseases healed, babies born, our first set of twins, three new missions established (Watford, Glasgow and lately Torry re-borne), many moved into their first homes, excellence in academics, great jobs, and many more. And what shall we say about that glorious miracle, the answer to the yearnings of many hearts who have cried at the sight of many magnificent church buildings turned into pubs, restaurants and nightclubs. Suddenly like the battle between David and Goliath, the Lord miraculously gave us victory over many developers and other bidders in the contest for what was the old Holburn Central parish of the Church of Scotland.

The original building was erected in 1836 in the record time of one year, a feat that earned the project leaders special commendation. The old church grew immensely and at a time, the membership was 3,000 and it was the third largest congregation of the Church of Scotland. Unfortunately matters went downhill so badly, that the entire church would be closed and building sold. We rejoice greatly for the privilege the Lord has given us in redeeming and handing the building over to us. One thing we are sure of, the glory of the latter house shall surpass that of the former. And to His glory, this altar shall keep burning until the Lord returns.

For the members, Christians, parishes and others from all over the world who gave and continue to give 'bricks' of all shapes and sizes to make the redemption possible, my prayer for you is simple but deep: The Lord will remember you for good, with favour and with mercy according to His great love, for the good you have done and continue to do towards His house. Your name and faithful deeds towards His house will not be blotted out! Amen!

This is the second edition of the magazine. Read it, enjoy it and be blessed. Pass around to others and enjoy the year 2008, the year that the Lord has made, the year and the season of the fisherman.

EDITORIAL FOR 2009
CITY OF GOD MAGAZINE
BY PASTOR MARK OSA IGIEHON

TELL ME ALL THE GREAT THINGS THAT THE LORD HAS BEEN DOING

And the king talked with the servant of God saying, Tell me, I pray thee, all the great things that the Lord has been doing…

I tell you and it is the truth, the whole truth and nothing but the truth and no one can contest it: the Lord has been doing great and marvellous things in our lives, in His Churches, across His kingdom, across the nations. We are overflowing with great reports of God's greatness: from Scotland, the United Kingdom, Europe and the nations.

When the king saw Gehazi, the servant of Elisha, the king was terribly excited and eagerly asked the servant of the man of God for the latest exciting reports of the doings of our great God. Gehazi started with the story of the Shunamite woman (2Kings 4.8-37, 8.1-6); but he did not complete his first report when lo and behold, the Shunamite, the daughter of God herself came into the King's Palace! Gehazi's did not have enough time to tell of the other wonderful reports: the prophet's widow and her little jar of oil with which she filled several containers; the twenty loaves that fed one hundred men.. What about the axe head that floated? And so on and so forth.

Gehazi's story telling was cut short so the king could go beyond hearing and become a participant in the living miracle that the Shunamite had become. There is somebody reading this who is being promoted from an observer to a partaker of miracles. Also, the Lord added once more to the chains of miracles that had become the hallmark and the lifestyle of the Shunamite woman.

The magazine you carry in your hand is loaded with great reports of what the Lord is doing across His kingdom, across lives, across churches, across the nations. Read it in excitement, read it prayerfully, read it with overflowing joy, read it with expectation, look for others with whom to share the great reports. Become a broadcaster for heaven under the unction of the Lord. I pray that, like the King, you will enter into your own miracles, you will become a participant, a beneficiary of the great goodness of the Lord of the universe and your joy will overflow.

Over the years the ministry has grown and every year at least one magazine is published. When the first edition of the magazine was published, the church ensured that every home in Torry got a copy. In addition, the magazine was widely distributed in Aberdeen, Scotland and the United Kingdom. This way, the gospel was spread abroad and a lot of people were clarified concerning the mission of the church. A lot of lives have been touched through this ministry and a lot of miracles occurred as a result, all to the Glory of God. The publication ministry, through magazines, was pioneered by Idongesit Umoh before his relocation to Ireland.

Idongesit Umoh

Another reason why the Magazine ministry was started was to aid the documentation of what God is doing in our midst. A famous British Politician and statesman known for his leadership during the Second World War once said:

""History will judge me well because I will write it" –Winston Churchill

Only documented history will be facts for tomorrow. This is the reason why the Magazine ministry is dedicated to recording what God is doing for His church, and through His church.

Recently, the magazine ministry has been assigned to document what God is doing in the Body of Christ locally and internationally.

THE MINISTRY OF BOOKS

In order to keep track of the lessons and secrets learnt from God, the ministry of books was started at Jesus House with the publishing house known as School of Wisdom Publishing House. The publishing house aims to communicate a comprehensive detailed account of what God has done in and through Jesus House Aberdeen. Another aim is to communicate the gospel of our Lord Jesus Christ in written form, through easy-to-read books that show forth God's mighty hand in our midst.

For as much as many have taken in hand to set forth in order a declaration of those things which are most surely believed among us, Even as they delivered them unto us, which from the beginning were eyewitnesses and ministers of the word; It seemed good to me also, having had perfect understanding of all things from the very first, to write unto thee in order, most excellent Theophilus, That thou mightest know the certainty of those things, wherein thou hast been instructed. – Luke 1.1-4(KJV)

As Luke the physician and apostle of our Lord Jesus Christ carefully recorded the ministry of our Lord Jesus Christ, we are keen on recording the dealings of God with His Church right from the inception for the people of our generation and generations to come.

Yet another reason why all these publications are done is as seen in the account of Gehazi in 2Kings8.4:

> *And the king talked with Gehazi the servant of the man of God, saying, Tell me, I pray thee, all the great things that Elisha hath done. - 2Kings 8.4 (KJV)*

The King asked the servant of Elisha to give him a full detail of what the Lord had done. In our world today, there are a lot of people and kings waiting to hear what the Lord is doing for us and through us. These are the things that will encourage them to come to the knowledge of God. If we do not document and relate the great testimonies of our God, the world would not know. Our testimony is our message and it is one effective tool God can use to change, transform and restore lives and relationships. We know the truth so we will share it to the Glory of God.

THE PARCHMENT

Apart from the magazines and books, the Lord has enabled the church to start up a book shop that makes available different materials that would help us in our Christian lives, answering many questions we may want to ask. This was started initially as a book stand when the church started in Torry. As the church grew, the demand for

STANDING BEFORE KINGS

'Seest thou a man diligent in his business? He shall stand before kings; he shall not stand before mean men' Proverbs 22:29

This proverb is being fulfilled in Jesus House as God granted favour to very diligent members of Jesus House.

BUCKINGHAM PALACE RECEPTION FOR FEMI, JH ABERDEEN MINISTER

One morning, Femi received a call inviting him for a reception by the Duke of Edinburgh (the Queen's husband) in recognition of his social work among the youth. This has to be crank call or a prank, he mused and was only convinced when the royal invitation letter arrived.

Though a very busy employee in a multinational oil company, Femi has created time to fulfil his calling as a minister in Jesus House Aberdeen and social work among youth such as giving career peptalks in schools. He was also the Nehemiah Project Coordinator whose zeal and faith sustained the drive to claim the Holburn Parish for Jesus House Aberdeen and for God.

Femi (R) with the Duke of Edinburgh

JH MUSIC DIRECTOR IS FINALIST FOR UK OIL & GAS AWARD

Obinna Njoku, an engineer in the oil and gas industry and the Music Director at Jesus House Aberdeen was one of three finalists nominated for the UK Oil & Gas Award of " Young Engineer of the Year". The high profile final had Scotland's First Minister, Alex Salmond and other bigwigs in attendance.

Obinna (2R) with Scotland's First Minister, Alex Salmond (3R) and John Gallagher, Shell VP (6R)

KACHI BAGS BEST M.SC STUDENT'S AWARD

The Lord, who said He will not owe any man, or woman crowned Onyedikachi's efforts with a distinction in her M.Sc. course at the University of Aberdeen and whats more, as one the best three graduating M.Sc. student!!! The picture on the right shows her receiving her award from Scotland's First Minister Alex Salmond. A diligent worker at Jesus House Aberdeen, for over 21 months Kachi made the long journey from Aberdeen to Inverness every Sunday or Saturday as part of the 5-man mission team to nurture the young Jesus House Inverness parish to its establishment.

Onyedikachi receiving Best Student Award from the First Minister

Group with lecturer

Best three M.Sc Students

THE CITY / GOD SUMMER 2008

City of God Magazine Extract (2008, page 20)

Christian literature grew. To the glory of God, on the acquisition of the church building, the book shop known as the Parchment was established. It has grown from strength to strength and the Lord has used it to bless a lot of lives within and outside the church. One of the achievements of the bookshop is the hosting of an annual movie night. This gives people the opportunity to come together, relax and listen to God's word as showcased in movies.

SECRETS FROM GOD'S CONSTRUCTION SITE

God demands appropriate documentation

Indeed, God expects us to keep a record of our dealings with him. Just as we keep diaries of our day to day life, our walk with God should be recorded. Not only is it useful to us, it is and can be useful to a friend, neighbour, family as well as future generations. Without a record of Christ's work on earth and those of His disciples and that of the prophets, we would not have had the bible and that might have adversely affected the spread of the Gospel.

Just as every nation has a documentation of their history, we need to document our encounters with God so that others can benefit from them. It may be asked: "Is the church a nation?" God in His Word refers to us as a royal priesthood, a holy nation and a peculiar people (1Peter2.9); so we are a nation.

Testimonies are essential for breakthroughs

Another lesson we have learnt is that God expects us to share our testimonies as they are essential tools for the realisation of other testimony.

From the life of Mary according to Luke 1.26-38, the Lord had a great blessing and testimony for her and it was that she was going to be the mother of the Saviour of the world who is Christ. Mary was a virgin and according to the physical laws, it was totally impossible for her to bear a child in that state. But in order that she would be convinced of God's promise, a testimony of a prior similarly impossible event was given her. This was the case of her cousin, Elisabeth, who at the time was considered barren and who had gone past the age of conception. Therefore, the news of her pregnancy was used as a sign of what God was about to do in Mary's life.

In our Christian walk, our testimony is all someone needs to hear to be encouraged and have faith that God is able to do all things. This is why we make His great deeds in our midst known through the magazines and different publications.

Testimonies are powerful weapons

And they overcame him by the blood of the Lamb and by the word of their testimony; and they loved not their lives unto the death. – Revelation 12.11

From the scripture above we have an understanding that our testimonies are weapons of spiritual warfare against the devil. Therefore, our testimonies are crucial tools for evangelism and spiritual warfare. This is so that when the devil and the people around us remind us of what might not seem right, we are quick to remind that we have overcome. Our testimonies give us assurance that if God has done miracles in other lives, He can do them in ours. This gives us assurance that God will fight our battles and do miracles time and again.

A practical example is seen in the life of David, when Saul asked him if he could fight Goliath. His testimony was this:

Thy servant kept his father's sheep, and there came a lion, and a bear, and took a lamb out of the flock: And I went out after him, and smote him, and delivered it out of his mouth: and when he arose against me, I caught him by his beard, and smote him, and slew him. Thy servant slew both the lion and the bear: and this un-circumcised Philistine shall be as one of them, seeing he hath defied the armies of the living God. – 1 Samuel 17. 34 – 36 (KJV)

This statement based on their faith and trust in God. He, indeed, delivered David from Goliath. This shows that our testimonies are a confirmation that God will always answer us.

Build an altar for divine encounters and testimonies.

In all our dealings with God, we have learnt that we should build an altar and a memorial unto God so that when we remember or see it, we would always give thanks to God.

And Jacob went out from Beer-sheba, and went toward Haran. And he lighted upon a certain place, and tarried there all night, because the sun was set; and he took of the stones of that place, and put them for his pillows, and lay down in that place to sleep. And he dreamed, and behold a ladder set up on the earth, and the top of it reached to heaven: and behold the angels of God ascending and descending on it. And, behold, the LORD stood above it, and said, I am the LORD God of Abraham thy father, and the God of Isaac: the land whereon thou liest, to thee will I give it, and to thy seed; And thy seed shall be as the dust of the earth, and thou shalt spread abroad to the west, and to the east, and to the north, and to the south: and in thee and in thy seed shall all the families of the earth be blessed. And, behold, I am with thee, and will keep thee in all places whither thou goest, and will bring thee again into this land; for I will not leave thee, until I have done that which I have spoken to thee of. And Jacob awaked out of his sleep, and he said, Surely the LORD is in this place; and I knew it not. And he was afraid, and said, How dreadful is this place! this is none other but the house of God, and this is the gate of heaven. And Jacob rose up early in the morning, and took the stone that he had put for his pillows, and set it up for a pillar, and poured oil upon the top of it. – Genesis 28.10-18 (KJV)

From the scripture above, after Jacob's encounter with God, he erected a memorial unto God commemorative of that encounter. He did the same when he encountered God in Peniel (Genesis 32.24-30). Encounters we have with God bring forth testimonies and it is needful to always build memorials around these testimonies and encounters.

■ CROSSOVER2010

■ CHURCH BREAKFAST MEETING
- JUNE 2007

INAUGURAL SERVICE AT CITY OF GOD

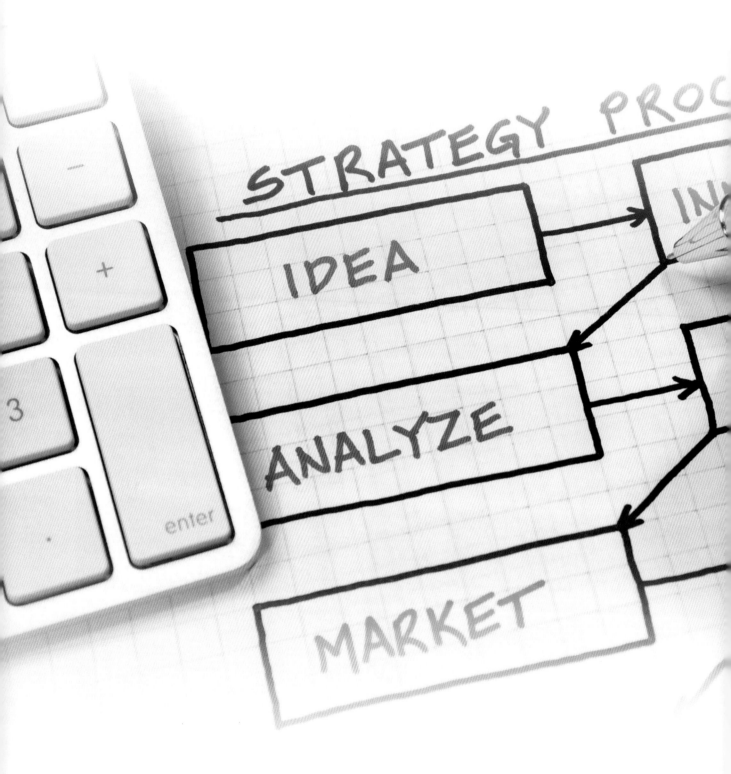

Chapter 11

THE GIFT OF ADMINISTRATORS

And in those days, when the number of the disciples was multiplied, there arose a murmuring of the Grecians against the Hebrews, because their widows were neglected in the daily ministration. Then the twelve called the multitude of the disciples unto them, and said, It is not reason that we should leave the word of God, and serve tables.

Wherefore, brethren, look ye out among you seven men of honest report, full of the Holy Ghost and wisdom, whom we may appoint over this business. But we will give ourselves continually to prayer, and to the ministry of the word. And the saying pleased the whole multitude: and they chose Stephen, a man full of faith and of the Holy Ghost, and Philip, and Prochorus, and Nicanor, and Timon, and Parmenas, and Nicolas a proselyte of Antioch: Whom they set before the apostles: and when they had prayed, they laid their hands on them. And the word of God increased; and the number of the disciples multiplied in Jerusalem greatly; and a great company of the priests were obedient to the faith. – Acts 6.1-7 (KJV)

In the early days, the work of the Lord in Jesus House so increased that the need arose for the church to set apart people who would take over the administration, so that the Pastor and the rest of the ministers would focus on prayers and ministry of the word, as it was in the early church according to Acts 6. 1-7. In order to avoid a repetition of the conflicts that arose prior to this action in the early church, an administrator was appointed in Jesus House. In the first year, Jimmy Akande faithfully oversaw church administration and in the following year Uzezi Okpokpor took over the responsibilities.

Then, in 2006, Tobi Ojuile became the accountant.

Uzezi continued in the administration of the work until her relocation to Nigeria. At that point, the entire administrative duty was handed over to Tobi who faithfully continued in the work of the Lord. She carried on until the church moved into her own building the City of God. Tobi became the first member of staff in the City of God building. The administrative work carried on until 2008, when she handed over the administrative oversight to Chidinma Oriunuebho.

As the church grew and the administrative responsibility increased, it became clear that more hands were needed in church administration. The first of such staff was Pearl Digwo as the Legal and Human Resource adviser, followed by Eniola Onafowokan as the Membership coordinator and Olorunnisola Okunuga as the Project Coordinator. These people have faithfully done the work of God, ensuring that the house of the Lord was professionally and adequately administered.

It is note-worthy that similar criteria used in the early church were used in selecting the administrative work force at the City of God. The criteria required that the administrators be: of honest report, and full of the Holy Ghost and wisdom. These characteristics are very important because these people work in the house of the Lord and need to be consecrated unto the Lord for His use.

Yet another reason for the appointment of administrators was to put the house of God in order as our God is a God of order. The standard and professionalism in the kingdom needs to astound the best of secular organisations.

The queen of Sheba heard about Solomon and his connection with the Name of God. She came to put his reputation to the test by asking tough questions. She made a grand and showy entrance into Jerusalem — camels loaded with spices, a huge amount of gold, and precious gems. She came to Solomon and talked about all the things that she cared about, emptying her heart to him. Solomon answered everything she put to him — nothing stumped him. When the queen of Sheba experienced for herself Solomon's wisdom and saw with her own eyes the palace he had built, the meals that were served, the impressive array of court officials and sharply dressed waiters, the lavish crystal, and the elaborate worship extravagant with Whole-Burnt-Offerings at the steps leading up to The Temple of God, it took her breath away. 1Kings 10.1-5 (The Message)

She said to the king, It was a true report I heard in my own land of your acts and sayings and wisdom. I did not believe it until I came and my eyes had seen. Behold, the half was not told me. You have added wisdom and goodness exceeding the fame I

Pictures from RCCG Scotland Women's Conference 2008

heard. Happy are your men! Happy are these your servants who stand continually before you, hearing your wisdom! Blessed be the Lord your God, Who delighted in you and set you on the throne of Israel! Because the Lord loved Israel forever, He made you king to execute justice and righteousness. And she gave the king 120 talents of gold and of spices a very great store and precious stones. Never again came such abundance of spices as these the queen of Sheba gave King Solomon. 1Kings 10.6-10 (KJV)

The biblical accounts above indicate that the queen of Sheba was so astonished in Solomon's day that she desired to know more about the house of God and the Kingdom of Solomon. She had heard a lot

about it and wanted to verify for herself. On getting to Solomon's kingdom, she was amazed at how orderly everything was: the impressive array of court officials and sharply dressed waiters, the elaborate worship and so on. Everything she saw was of the best standard obtainable. This came as a result of proper administration indicating clearly that Solomon's kingdom had an excellent administrative team.

This is another reason why the administrative team has been set up. To help the pastor and ministers to ensure everything is in order and running smoothly, all to the Glory of God. As it is recorded, good administration was one of the reasons that led the Queen of Sheba to bless the name of the Lord God of Solomon. This is also one of the principles that we hold on to and are constantly improving upon; so that through excellent administration and order of service, unbelievers will be amazed and subsequently come to the saving knowledge of the Lord Jesus.

The church administration has a church Secretary, Iyiola Ogedengbe who is the Minister in charge of workers and members administration. He ensures that everything regarding the workforce is done appropriately to the Glory of God and that the church workers are well managed, administered to and trained to professionally acceptable standards. With these trainings, everything is done in order according to the will of God and according to the mandate and mission statement of the church.

THE BOARD OF TRUSTEES

Another set of people whom the Lord has used to adequately manage the affairs of the church are the 'Trustees'. Originally, the board included Jimi Akande, Uzezi Obaro-Okpokpor, Alero Igiehon, Obinna Njoku and Pastor Mark Igiehon; with Femi Akarakiri joining the board later on. Today the board of trustees include Obinna Njoku, Alero Igiehon, Dapo Olanrewaju, Pastor Mark Igiehon and Wilfred Emmanuel who is the chairman of the board.

THE BUSINESS TEAM

As the church grew, the need for improved levels of professionalism during our outreaches became pertinent, hence the institution of the Business Team. This team consisting of Edosa Akioya, Yinka Jimoh, Joe Ochie, Tosin Emilolorun and Obinna Njoku perform roles similar to makeup artists backstage. They work on giving the outreaches a professional touch, ensuring that the marketing of these events are well done. Furthermore, they ensure that the right message and picture for each intended outreach is aptly passed across to the target audiences.

To the glory of God, they have been able to bring their wealth of experience to the annual 'Battle of The Bands" event which looks at rewarding young artist and the organisation of the Aberdeen Mass choir concerts. They are involved in the Smithfield property and other building project(s); actively responsible for the development of the business plan for new church projects

PENIEL

Every year, the church holds a conference known as PENIEL. PENIEL is the foremost Christian conference in the City of Aberdeen hosted by Jesus House @ City of God Aberdeen. The convention is loaded with bible expositions, prophetic impartation, revelations of the Word backed up by an overflow of healings and deliverance as well as uplifting soul gospel music. The conference is inspired by the encounter of Jacob whose life was transformed at Peniel.

The conference has grown to be a huge event from its little beginnings in July 2006 at Aberdeen Beach ballroom. Today Peniel has grown from a weekend conference to a 10 day conference and the Testimonies abound.

Pictures from PENIEL conference

Pictures from PENIEL conference

SECRETS FROM GOD'S CONSTRUCTION SITE

God is orderly

One of the vital lessons we have are learning about God is that He is orderly and delighted when He see us doing things in an orderly fashion, bringing glory to His name.

Order brings increase

Our journey has shown that order in the house of God brings increase. In Acts 6 for example, the early church had challenges with the order and administration. When that was addressed, the Word of the Lord increased and the number of the disciples multiplied greatly.

And the word of God increased; and the number of the disciples multiplied in Jerusalem greatly; and a great company of the priests were obedient to the faith. — Acts 6.7 (KJV)

The Lord brought increase to the church when the issues of her administration were addressed. In the same way, when the administration of our individual lives and in God's present day church is executed appropriately, the Lord will increase us greatly on every side.

Pictures from PENIEL conference

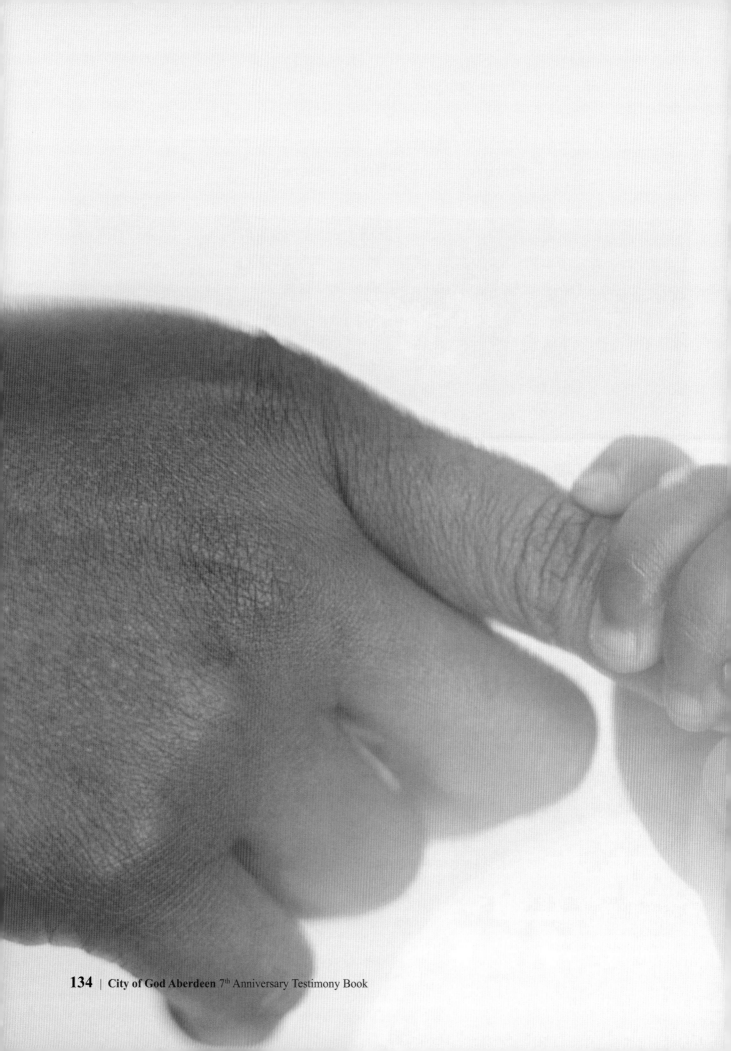

Chapter 12

THANK GOD FOR GOOD PARENTS

The origin of life, its existence and survival has a source from which it originates and has life. This source of origin, known as the parent, through reproduction gives birth to the organism. Parents are known for their support and training during the developmental stages of the organism. Jesus House Aberdeen has God as the source to its existence.

However, Jesus House Port Harcourt, a parish of the Redeemed Christian Church of God, is the physical parents through which the church was birthed. As earlier mentioned in the first chapter, Pastor Mark was commissioned and supported to start the church in Aberdeen through Jesus House Port Harcourt, Nigeria.

A lot of Pastors from the parent church has been of great support to the church in Aberdeen including Pastors Charles Adegoke, Songo Barango, Ray Eli, Kola Bolanta, Jide Odunlami, Rosemary Odunlami, and Sonny Wogu.

st. Agu Irukwu, Pst. Andrew Adeleke and Pst. Kola Bamigbade, the three members of the RCCG U K Executive Council with Pst. Mrs Modupe Afolabi, the Executive Administrator of RCCG Central Office UK

Pastor Wilfred Emmanuel, Pastor Alero Igiehon and Pastor Roseline Emmanuel

Pastor Charles Adegoke

SHORT HISTORY OF JESUS HOUSE PORT HARCOURT, NIGERIA
(ADAPTED FROM A DECADE OF DIVINE GRACE BY JESUS HOUSE PORT HARCOURT)

The history and story of Jesus House Port Harcourt is like the proverbial mustard seed, the smallest of all, yet able to grow to a mighty oak tree! The Jesus House Port Harcourt started in 1996.

Early the previous year (1995), the Redeemed Christian Church of God, King's Palace (the mother parish) opened a House fellowship centre in the residence of Brother and Sister George Ezekwem within Rumuibekwe Estate, the House Fellowship centre grew and flourished and there arose a need to plant a parish within the vicinity of the Estate so that the members of the House Fellowship would not have to travel to King's Palace which was quite a distance from Rumuibekwe.

Meanwhile, before it became apparent that a parish needed to be established in this locality, Pastor Tony Abel - Tariah had received a vision to plant a church in the area. He was then the Pastor-in-charge of King's Palace, he began to make the necessary contacts and by the first quarter of 1996, some properties had been secured including a parcel of land to build on and construction started. In this regard, we note the support and sacrifice of Pastor Shyngle Wigwe, an Elder in the Redeemed Christian Church of God who allowed the church to use his personal house situated behind the church auditorium to accommodate the children, teenagers and also the administrative offices for the church. After so many years of use, Pastor Wigwe graciously permitted the church to acquire the property from him and this is the site on which the construction of the new building project is about to commence. The building is proposed to accommodate the Provincial Secretariat, Teenage church and children's church.

The story of Jesus House Port Harcourt is yet another confirmation of the scripture that says 'never despise the days of humble beginnings.' From an uncompleted building and a congregation of less than 100 worshippers, have grown to a parish of 4000, becoming in the process of time an Area Headquarters, then a Zonal Headquarters, a Mega Stand alone Parish and now the Provincial Headquarters of the Redeemed Christian Church of God Province 3.

The inaugural service of Jesus House was held on December 14, 1996. Since then, Jesus House Port Harcourt has remained 'unstoppable'. Our good Lord has used several men and women to move forward His work in our midst.

Jesus House Port Harcourt has an apostolic mandate and torch to reach our environment and the world for Christ. Till date, we have planted churches in and outside Nigeria.

PASTOR CHRIS GBENLE AND FOUNTAIN OF LOVE FAMILY

PASTOR CHRIS GBENLE

Another characteristic of parents is that they might not be physically involved in the birthing of the organism but involved in supporting the organism at different points in time during the development process. Apart from Jesus House Port Harcourt, a number of people have also served as parents to the church. One of such is the Fountain of Love Church under the pastoral leadership of Pastor Chris Gbenle. Fountain of Love was the church Pastor Mark attended in Aberdeen until he set out to start a Jesus House Parish. This church has been of tremendous support to Jesus House Aberdeen.

Once when Pastor Chris Gbenle was asked about the impact of the Redeemed Christian Church of God in Scotland, this was his remark:

"I will start with the major landmarks of the forward movements that we have made...Numerical growth, planting of other parishes, acquiring property. These are all positive impacts or influences in the city. I remember when I first came here the spiritual atmosphere was not like this. The prayer initiative that we have every month has resulted in testimonies and even other churches are feeling our impact...Definitely the city is being covered by prayers. By the grace of God, a lot has changed. There are various initiatives we are pursuing at Jesus House and here at the Fountain of Love like the Faith Clinic, Thank-God-its-Friday and many other programs. All these things are like seeds being sown. I can assure us, by the grace of God that all the previous efforts have yielded results as we can see today. So let us not be weary in doing well because in due time we shall reap the results if we faint not."

We must also give a special recognition to Pastor Wilfred and Roseline Emmanuel. They are part and parcel of the Jesus House family. Pastor Wilfred is the chairman of the Board of Trustees of RCCG Jesus House Aberdeen. We thank God for our wonderful elder Ron Fake and family.

RCCG CENTRAL OFFICE AND EXECUTIVE COUNCIL UK

The Redeemed Christian Church of God's Central Office in the United Kingdom has also been of tremendous support to the Jesus House Aberdeen. They have been very supportive in counselling the church as the church grew. In the Central Office, Pastor Modupe Afolabi and Pastor Agu Irukwu have supported the church especially in arranging for the General Overseer of the Redeemed Christian Church of God, Pastor E. A. Adeboye to dedicate the City of God Complex. Another set of people who Jesus House regard as parents are the Executive Council of Redeemed Christian Church of God in the United Kingdom ably headed by Pastor Agu Irukwu. Other members are Pastor Andrew Adeleke and Pastor Kola Bamgbade with Pastor Modupe Afolabi as Executive Administrator.

JESUS HOUSE MINISTRY PARTNERS

It is note-worthy to mention that a couple of ministers from different RCCG parishes and other ministries have been precious partners and continue to support the church in prayers, counsel and parenting. They include Reverend Samson and Reverend Mrs Stella Ajetomobi, Reverend and Reverend Mrs David Omo-Osemwengie, Reverend Lyndsay Mann, Pastor Dotun Ojelabi, Pastor Peter Olawale, Pastor and Pastor Mrs. Olumide, Pastor Anda Baiye, Reverend George Adegboye, Pastor John Holme, Pastor Olu Rotimi, Pastor Steve Okwosa, Pastor Mark Stone, Pastor Joe Ibojie, Reverend and Reverend Mrs John McPhee, Reverend John Ilocgben, Evangelist Gboyega Shitta, and Bishop Etidia.

Pictures from the Jesus House Gamaliel (Lawyers and Commercial) Forum

SECRETS FROM GOD'S CONSTRUCTION SITE

Foundations are important

Our foundation is very vital to the success of our life and achievements. As a child grows, different activities are provided by the parents to encourage weaning, growth and development. As a church we saw the motherly care and support of Jesus House Port Harcourt which guided the church in growth.

In all we do, we learn to give ourselves and our children the right atmosphere for growth and development.

If the foundation is destroyed what can the righteous do?

This is a question God is putting to us His children as a reminder of the importance attached to our foundation. Therefore, we have to make adequate effort to ensure that we are built on the solid and right foundation which is Jesus Christ.

God wants us to honour our parents

Giving honour to one's parents is very essential, important and it is the first command from God with a promise.

Honour thy father and thy mother:
that thy days may be long upon the land which the LORD thy God giveth thee. Exodus 20.12 (KJV)

It is only when we honour our parents that the Lord prolongs our days. This is the reason why we have dedicated this chapter to honour those who are our parents as a church.

Parents are duty-bound to chastise the kids

We have learnt that it is the responsibility of parents to chastise their children when they deviate from the right principles. This is very important because when parents cannot chastise their children, they become bastards.

If ye endure chastening, God dealeth with you as sons: for what son is he whom the father chasteneth not? But if ye be without chastisement, whereof all are partakers, then are ye bastards, and not sons. Heb 12.8 (KJV)

Therefore, to be true children of God we ought to have a parental figure covering to correct us when we go astray; otherwise, we make ourselves bastards.

Chapter 13

AND TO THE UTTERMOST PARTS OF THE WORLD

But ye shall receive power, after that the Holy Ghost is come upon you: and ye shall be witnesses unto me both in Jerusalem, and in all Judaea, and in Samaria, and unto the uttermost part of the earth. – Acts 1.8 (KJV)

And Jesus came and spake unto them, saying, All power is given unto me in heaven and in earth. Go ye therefore, and teach all nations, baptizing them in the name of the Father, and of the Son, and of the Holy Ghost: Teaching them to observe all things whatsoever I have commanded you: and, lo, I am with you always, even unto the end of the world. Amen. – Matthew 28.18-20 (KJV)

On Jesus' departure from earth to heaven, He gave His disciples a charge to go and be witnesses unto him in Jerusalem, in Judaea and in Samaria and unto the uttermost part of the earth. This charge was then passed unto us to carry on the mantle of evangelism. Our Jerusalem refers to our base or city and moving further to the uttermost part of the earth.

As a church, we started in Aberdeen and to the Glory of God we have four churches in Aberdeen and in most cities in Scotland. Then, we moved to reaching out to the uttermost part of the earth. Today we have missions/churches planted in Paris, Rouen, Le Havre, Marseilles, Watford, Wick and Hungary.

EGLISE FRANCAIS

In Jesus House, in other to reach everyone, a French church was started in City of God, Aberdeen with Zoe Gbahi as coordinator. The aim is to cater for the people who speak French and would love to have their church service in French. It is also to cater for members who would like to learn French or improve their French.

JESUS HOUSE ROUEN,
- Winning the battle of Normandy

Normandy in France is popular as the landing point for Allied force in the Second World War. Centuries earlier, a nephew of the English King by name William the Conqueror who rules Normandy invaded England to claim the English Throne. To the Glory of God, we have been opportune to be His labourer in Rouen, Normandy to bring people back to Christ.

Jesus House Rouen was established by Pastor Mike Dada (now Pastor, CoG Watford) in 2005 and has been winning the spiritual battle for the souls in the Normandy region and France. Indeed the church has blossomed and matured.

Testimonies abound of God's goodness: A fully equipped Church auditorium and office was dedicated by the RCCG Regional Coordinator in Europe Mainland.

Others include the spiritual growth of members, new church bus, new babies, and several other testimonies. Every Tuesday, the Church holds its flagship program "The Solution Hour".

In other to ensure that the mission work to the uttermost parts is well managed, a mission team was formed, led by Sis Dolapo Mainassara Faturoti. This team is in charge of church planting in the different parts of Europe. They visit the churches in Europe and ensure that the churches are not lacking in any form. They are also involved in prayers for the churches in Europe. To the Glory of God the team has been indeed amazing as the churches are doing great, healthy and waxing strong every day. A lot of testimonies have come from these outreaches in Europe and indeed, God continues to be glorified.

Jesus House Budapest

TESTIMONY REPORT

Letter to God by Prison Inmate

(Inverness prison)

God the Father, God the Son,
God the Holy Ghost
Please be with me, in this
place I call my home
It's not easy being a Christian
as You can see.

When people tell me
the apple never falls far from the tree
I sit here in prison alone in my cell
While my family and friends have
walked away and left me in here,
to deal with this pain.

Lord, everything I had to my
name has been taken away
Lord, You have shown me the price
that I must pay for me to understand why
You died on the cross so I can be born again
You died on the cross of Your own free will
But thank you especially for dying for me.

Lord, there are a lot of things
I don't understand.
But please show me and guide
Me with Your loving hands
I don't know what the future
will hold on where I go.
But thank you for saving my soul

SECRETS FROM GOD'S CONSTRUCTION SITE

We MUST preach the gospel

18And Jesus came and spake unto them, saying, All power is given unto me in heaven and in earth. 19Go ye therefore, and teach all nations, baptizing them in the name of the Father, and of the Son, and of the Holy Ghost: 20Teaching them to observe all things whatsoever I have commanded you: and, lo, I am with you always, even unto the end of the world. Amen. – Matthew 28.18-20 (KJV)

On Jesus' departure to Heaven after His ministry on earth, He gave us the commission to go into the world and teach the nations the gospel. Therefore, we have to go out and preach the gospel where ever we find ourselves. It is a command that we have to obey. Another thing we learn from the above scriptures is that He will always be with us, no matter what. He has us in His hands and would guard us, so we do not need to be afraid or scared of going out to preach and teach people of God's love.

Jesus' return depends on us

During Jesus Christ's ministry on earth, He made His church understand that He would not return for the church until the gospel has been preached all over the world. Hence, it is our duty to ensure that we evangelise to as many people as possible; as our delay would delay Jesus' return. We are therefore encouraged not to lose heart but to keep on preaching the gospel of our Lord Jesus Christ.

Chapter 14

ORGANIC GROWTH

Growth has been defined as an increase in some quantity over time. This can be physical for example increase in height, size or length. It can also be abstract, for example an organism becoming more mature. On the other hand, organic growth is the process of business expansion due to increased output, sales, or both.

In Jesus house we can say that the Lord has equally increased us over time. Physically, the church started with six people and the Lord has increased us mightily that we cannot comprehend it. He has increased us greatly by bringing a lot of people into the church to His glory. Our testimony is that God has been good. At the beginning of Jesus House Aberdeen, one of the prayers that has been and is still prayed for is that there will be growth.

Some people pray for the fruit of the womb and have waited but the Lord has not made that to be our case. In 2004 when the church started, the first baby was added to the family of Bro Azu Usuagwu. After that addition, the church has never ceased to have a birth to celebrate regularly. The Lord has preserved both the mothers and babies all to the Glory of God.

MARRIAGES

Another form of increase that has always been in the prayers of Pastor Mark Igiehon is that the Lord will bless us in terms of relationships. To the Glory of God, the Lord has preserved marriages in Jesus House.

Photos of Weddings

Photos of Babies and Dedication

MARRIAGE AND HEBREW WOMEN COUNSELLING

Another arm that the Lord has used to bring growth in the church is the counselling team on marriage and pregnant/ waiting mothers. A lot of work goes into counselling to maintain relationships and to prepare couples for life time partnerships. The counselling team comprising of seasoned ministers silently work to see the growth and strengthening of relationships, all to the glory of God. The Marriage counselling team is coordinated by Alero Igiehon.

PHOTOS FROM COUPLES BREAKFAST

The Hebrew women team is coordinated by Mummy Femi Labeodan. They organise weekly prayer meetings for pregnant women and those believing God for the fruit of the womb. Their meetings are always a time of praise, prayer, testimonies and strengthening through the Word of God

COUPLES' BREAKFAST

In other to ensure that the sweet wine in the marriages of the members does not turn bitter, the couple's breakfast was initiated. This is set out for couples to come together, have a good time and renew their relationships. They learn more about each other and learn how to make their relationships better and glorious, all to the Glory of God. The Couples breakfast is coordinated by Onyedikachi Zubi-Emele and her husband Zubi Emele. It is held once in a quarter and a lot of lives and marriages have benefited and are been blessed by it.

PASTORAL COUNSELLING

In other to ensure growth of members and families, the church has a team of ministers that are dedicated to counselling people on the issues of life. The counsels they give are based on the word of God. The team is coordinated by Pastor Mark Igiehon and Niyi Adebayo. They selflessly together with other ministers open themselves to people freely, giving counsel to the glory of God.

A Team's Good life meeting at Bar ICI 2007

A section of the first LMU seminar 2008

Pastor Niyi and Dapo conducting baptism 2008

A-TEAM

Another prayer and heart desire is that the Lord would cause the singles to find their spouse in the church. At first people thought it was a joke. To this end, a team was formed called A-Team for singles and youths. The team is by Ogechi Aguma. The team organises events for Christian singles to meet, mingle, and study the word. This is to develop themselves in their careers, relationships and spiritual lives. Through this group the Lord has divinely cause brethren to meet their spouses. In 2009, the church experienced a breaking forth of godly marriages and go-

ing forward, we believe God for a greater harvest of godly marriages to the Glory of God.

LOVE AND MARRIAGE UNIVERSITY (LMU)

In 2009, the LMU was started. This was an initiative by Pastor Mark Igiehon. This university is different from what we have in the world today. This looks at teaching young people what is required in preparation for marriage and how to go about marriage. It also encourages young people to pray for their spouse even if they have not met the person. Another reason the LMU has been formed is to address any wrong perception of marriage and relationships in the world today. The wrong perception has destroyed a lot of lives and the LMU intends to reverse this trend that has equally crept into the church, resulting in high divorce rate. The LMU also is for married people as it teaches on marriages and how to protect our spouses and how to make our marriages, a "marriage made in heaven". The University is coordinated by Mr and Mrs Okerinde..

In the future, we trust God as a church to expand this ministry so that the government and the world will come to us to seek knowledge and wisdom on how to make their marriages solid and divorce proof. This way we can reach out to them and minister to them about the good news of the Gospel.

PHOTOS OF THE DIFFERENT PARISHES

City of God Glasgow with Pastor Kola Bolanta 2007

Elgin Church

City of God Watford 2008

J H Inverness church at PENIEL 2006 in Aberdeen

Edinburgh Tabernacle at lunch

JH Budapest at a church service

JH Inverness with Provincial Pastor 2008

JH Paris at a church service

Through these groups, the Lord has brought increase in His church and caused the church to grow rapidly in seven (7) years all to the Glory of God. The Lord has also increased His church and has enabled us plant churches in different parts of Scotland and Europe as a whole. To the glory of God, we have been able to plant parishes in:

- Aberdeen (City of God), Scotland
- Aberdeen (Dyce), Scotland
- Aberdeen (Hilton), Scotland
- Aberdeen (Torry), Scotland
- Edinburgh, Scotland
- Elgin, Scotland
- Glasgow, Scotland
- Inverness, Scotland
- Montrose, Scotland
- Perth, Scotland
- Stirling, Scotland
- Wick, Scotland
- Watford, England
- Paris, France
- Rouen, France
- Marseille, France
- Le Havre, France
- Budapest, Hungary

Another aspect of growth is in terms of maturity. We can say that the Lord has matured us as individuals and as a church. To the Glory of God, most of the planted missions are standing on their own both in administration and in ministering. We acknowledge that only God could have done it all. As a body the Lord has increased us all round.

TESTIMONY REPORT

SCOTLAND: A CAPTURE OF THE BEAUTY OF GOD'S CREATION

by: Kenechukwu Njoku

Never have I been in a scary yet trilling journey the one I had to Wick three years ago for a music outreach programme. The trip ended up in an awesome adventure which revealed to us the beauty of God's creation within the highlands of Scotland.

Scotland is indeed beautiful and a place where you could appreciate nature and the creativity of our God. We did not intend to use the tourists' route, but ended up there and were surprisingly embraced with so much memorable attractions.

On the 24th of August 2008, I, my husband and some of our church members embarked on a journey to Wick. We were to stop over in Inverness and continue on our trip with some of our brethren in Inverness. While we were not 100% certain about the direction, we trusted our satellite navigator to take us to our destination.

What we did not know was that the navigator has several route options in getting there.

Apparently, we had mistakenly programmed the navigator to follow the country road to Inverness, and that was where the dramatic journey began.

We left Aberdeen city centre and in about ten minutes, we were in a roundabout approaching Westhill. Then the navigator instructed us to turn off to the left to a single lane, country road. Although we were a bit surprised, we were hoping to be out to motorway soon, but that did not happen.

The further we got into the road, the more we realised that we were not getting close to any motorway. We also did not see much houses, except a few that looked like old castles, no petrol stations, (thank God we filled the petrol tank before our take off), and hardly any vehicle. We realized that the road was very winding and sloppy, sometimes tilted to an angle and just few inches out of the road was a river, a pond or even a deep gully! We also saw a sign that says 'Beware of Deers'! None of us had ever been in such a road and we knew we needed much caution while driving. We were concerned about visibility as it was gradually getting dark and we needed to get out of the country road before it got really dark.

Gripped with tension, I found myself muttering all manner of prayers, including speaking in tongues most especially when we had to drive up through the very high and steep hills as well as descend down the hills. As we drove up the hills, we eventually found out that we got high up that we could see the third clouds just above us. I could also feel a bit of pressure in my ears due to the high altitude, as if I was in an aeroplane. Looking down the hills, we could see the beautiful landscapes covered with different shades and colours of plants and trees, farmlands, curves of river paths and the winding road curves. Because we went so high we came across snow up in the hills, although it not yet winter. We also went by a skiing resort. Up on the hills, the trees laid beautifully arranged, some were covered with patches of grasses. In between the trees and grasses were road curves like the ones which we were on. We could also see the beautiful farmlands and on a closer view, were grazing cattle and sheep on them. Indeed, that was really lovely scenery. The whole combination looked very attractive and breathe taking. It looked like one of the most beautiful paintings I ever saw, which was captured in a portrait. That memory still remains with me till today, although, unfortunately, I was more interested in reaching my destination than trying to find out more about where we were, so I did not get details of these places.

After, over three hours of ramming over the hills and through trees and dodging side gullies, ponds, rivers and valleys, we eventually emerged on a free dual carriage motor way and we thanked God for safety. We then joined our other brethren in a larger vehicle in Inverness, in another two hours trip to Wick, a town which lie in the east coast of northern Scotland. That on its own was another incredible journey.

On this journey, we discovered that tourist used to come and camp there, because we could see some caravans for hire even within that remote route! For me, I think it was worth it. The journey was amazing, we had a great time and on our way back we stopped by at different tourist attractions including the Don Robin Castle in the Highlands.

Pictures from Wick Trip from Wick Trip

Mission Team at Don Robin Castle

Mission Team on their way back to Aberdeen

SECRETS FROM GOD'S CONSTRUCTION SITE

God wants us to grow

One of the lessons we have learnt as a church is that God wants us to grow. As individuals as well, God does not want us to keep being at one place but he wants us to grow in all we do: our word knowledge, prayer life, career and everything that concerns us. He does not want us to remain in one position for a long while.

Growth must be unto maturity

As newborn babes, desire the sincere milk of the word, that ye may grow thereby – 1 Peter 2.2 (KJV)

Of whom we have many things to say, and hard to be uttered, seeing ye are dull of hearing. For when for the time ye ought to be teachers, ye have need that one teach you again which be the first principles of the oracles of God; and are become such as have need of milk, and not of strong meat. For every one that useth milk is unskilful in the word of righteousness: for he is a babe. But strong meat belongeth to them that are of full age, even those who by reason of use have their senses exercised to discern both good and evil. – Hebrews 5.11-14 (KJV)

Not only does God want us to grow, but he wants us to mature. In 1Peter2.2, God wants us to desire the sincere milk of the word of God. However, He does not want us to stop at the milk. Rather, as His children, he wants us to grow from drinking milk to eating strong meat. Like our earthly children, we want them to move from taking milk to eating solid food and so does our heavenly father. He wants us to grow to maturity in our walk with Him. It is only at this point of maturity that he can hand over great kingdom business to us. It is only then that we can partake fully in all He has for us as His children.

A physical example is seen when a child is born, the parents give him toys but as the child grows and matures the parents begin to entrust into their hands things of greater value. Rather than a toy phone, they will give a real phone. Rather than a toy car, they give a real car. So does God want to entrust things of value in our care.

God wants us to reproduce

I am the true vine, and my Father is the husbandman. Every branch in me that beareth not fruit he taketh away: and every branch that beareth fruit, he purgeth it, that it may bring forth more fruit. – John 15. 1-2 (KJV)

Ye have not chosen me, but I have chosen you, and ordained you, that ye should go and bring forth fruit, and that your fruit should remain: that whatsoever ye shall ask of the Father in my name, he may give it you. –John 15. 16 (KJV)

Above growing and getting matured in the things of God, He wants us to bear fruits. He says in the book of John that He is the true vine and we are the branches. He expects us to bear fruits since we are a part of Him. Not only do we bear fruits but that our fruits should abide. If in any way we do not bear fruits or our fruits do not abide then we are not of Him.

Bearing fruit means reproducing Christ in us in the lives of others. It also refers to achieving great things. If we call ourselves His and we are not excelling in the things we do, then there is a problem. Hence, we need to bear fruit to His glory. That is why we are created; to be fruitful. After the creation of man in God's image, this is what God did:

And God blessed them, and God said unto them, Be fruitful, and multiply, and replenish the earth, and subdue it: and have dominion over the fish of the sea, and over the fowl of the air, and over every living thing that moveth upon the earth. – Genesis 1. 28 (KJV)

When man fell, we lost that power but Jesus came and restored us back to our original state. Hence, we have to be fruitful and our fruits have to abide to the Glory of God.